everything
jet organized
nd sanity at
run, and in
$12.95
ocm67945584

I Hate Filing

I HATE FILING

*Everything You Need to
Get Organized for Success
and Sanity at Home,
on the Run and in the Office*

SHARON MANN

President of the I Hate Filing Club

Health Communications, Inc.
Deerfield Beach, Florida

www.hcibooks.com

**Library of Congress Cataloging-in-Publication Data
is available at the Library of Congress**

©2006 Sharon Mann
ISBN 0-7573-0395-1

Publisher: Health Communications, Inc.
          3201 S.W. 15th Street
          Deerfield Beach, FL 33442-8190

Cover design by Larissa Hise Henoch
Inside book design by Lawna Oldfield Patterson
Inside book formatting by Dawn Von Strolley Grove

I would like to dedicate this book to my son Marc. He was the inspiration and the sole purpose for me getting my ACT together. As an adult, he continues to inspire me.

A special thank you to my husband Ivan for not only being my best friend, but for believing in me when at times, I had my own doubts.

This book could not have been made possible without the I Hate Filing Club team for all of the help with the newsletters and special projects. And last but certainly not least, a big thank you to Mike Pucci and Michael "Smo" Smollins.

Contents

Introduction

Getting Things in Order

This is my story of how organization helped one young mom go from surviving to thriving.

Most of us are far too young to remember the original comedy routines of Laurel and Hardy. Yet, through the timelessness of videos and television reruns, most of us know the scoop—they always seem to get themselves in over their heads, until Oliver Hardy wryly utters the memorable words to Stan Laurel: "Well, this is another fine mess . . ."

Sound familiar? The fact is that millions of people find themselves in the midst of a mess at some point in their lives, a mess that is no laughing matter. For many, the difference between rising above the challenge and thriving despite adversity can be summed up in a single word—organization.

When life throws you a curve ball, one of the best ways to

overcome the challenge and turn potential failure into success is
to organize your priorities. An important part of getting your life
in order involves emphasizing the positives and concentrating on
the opportunities, whether it's taking control of your office and
desk before it takes over your life or learning how to pay your
bills on time. By utilizing those strategies, chances are your
future will be filled with the kind of personal and professional
growth you've envisioned.

Such is the case with me, an organizational and productivity
expert for a global office supplies company. I am the president of
the Pendaflex® I Hate Filing Club, which has more than one
hundred thousand members. The club offers timely advice,
insightful tips and valuable expertise for people who want to
become more successful in corporate offices and more organized
in their home offices, at school and in life as a whole. To see all
that I have achieved at this point in my life cannot truly be
appreciated without realizing what a disorganized mess my life
had become just a few short years ago. It's a story that hundreds
of thousands of women and men can relate to.

At the age of thirty, I was faced with the prospect of starting
my life all over again. I found myself in the middle of a divorce
with my five-month-old son to care for. Having very few options,
I sold my house, moved into an apartment with my infant son
and returned to the work force in order to support the two of us.
It seemed as if, suddenly, my life had turned upside down and
chaotic beyond description. Not only couldn't I see the

proverbial "light at the end of the tunnel," but I couldn't even see the train coming down the tracks. The need to juggle a myriad of responsibilities was overwhelming. I remained determined, however, and somehow managed to strike a balance between raising a child, starting a new career and putting food on the table in our new home.

Following the divorce, I had to figure out a way to make it all work, and the best way to accomplish this was to organize a strict but manageable routine for my son and me. Up to this point in my life I had not been very organized. I can remember a day in high school when I want to school wearing two different color shoes. When I first got married I needed to put a sign at the door reminding me to take dinner out of the freezer before leaving for work. And more times than not, I still forgot and ended up scrambling some eggs for dinner. But things were different now, and my new lifestyle was calling out—no *screaming*—for organization.

One of my first big dilemmas was that I would need someone to watch Marc while I went to work. Considering all my options (which were frighteningly few), I reached out to, of all people, my ex-mother-in-law. Now before you all raise your eyebrows and sigh out loud, just know that what I did was to create an arrangement that would be a win-win-win for everyone in the end.

Each day, I left bright and early from my home in the Riverdale section of the Bronx, drove to my ex-mother-in-law's house in Yonkers to drop my son off, and then make the difficult commute to Manhattan where my job was located. At the end of the day, I returned to Yonkers, picked up my son and continued home to my apartment in Riverdale. I made dinner (thank goodness for macaroni and cheese), spent quiet time with my son and then prepared him for bed. The arrangement, although very demanding, worked out for everyone. My son and his grandmother got to spend time together, which created a lifelong bond between the three of us.

Although I was able to overcome the daunting obstacle of finding someone to babysit Marc during the day and had a daily routine, I had to keep it all together by keeping the house organized. This way Marc and I could spend quality time together, and making sure that he went to bed the same time every night made for an easier time getting ready in the morning. I, like so many women who have experienced the challenges of being a single mother, will tell you that the situation at times made me feel like giving up. But I did not give up; instead, I was driven to take my life to another level of success. Drawing upon previous experiences I had gained in the sales and customer service fields, I became a highly successful textile sales representative in the garment center located in midtown Manhattan. I then moved on to become a marketing manager and then a customer service manager. Having an organized routine kept me from leaving home with cereal in my lap and a child's toy in my coat pocket—and it helped me focus on work when at work and focus on home when at home. And believe it or not, being organized helped me have

a social life. Eventually I got remarried to a wonderful support-
ive man.

Through organization, I found not only peace of mind, but
the ability to accomplish everything I needed to. It gave me a
sense of empowerment. I felt powerful, in control and able to
take on whatever life sent my way. Anything I wanted was within
my reach after I established a sense of organization in the office
and at home.

Turning chaos into a success story was not easy for me. Yet, by
taking an organized approach I was able to do much more than
get my life in order—I made it better.

In addition to being the president of the Pendaflex® I Hate
Filing Club (*www.ihatefilingclub.com*), I am also an Organizational
Expert for the company, one of the world's leading makers of
innovative office solutions. And I'm here to help you get organized. In this book, I will help you overcome the mundane and the
extraordinary. In fact, I will help you learn that organizing the
mundane leads to extraordinary things.

The info, tips, tricks and tools you'll unearth in the following
pages are straight from the club archives, and they can—and
will—help you transform your life. Organization *can* help you
accomplish your goals, whether you want to get ahead in your
career or better manage life's inevitable details. And best of all,
this book makes getting (and staying) organized easier than you
ever thought possible! The answers to self-empowerment and
organization are all right here.

CHAPTER 1

WHAT ORGANIZATION MEANS TO ME

It's Time to Get Your "ACT" Together

Where do you need organization in your life? Take a look at the following tips and see if you're I Hate Filing Club material.

✓ Do you wake up in the middle of the night remembering that you forgot to do an important task earlier in the day?

✓ Did you buy something, only to find that you already own it?

✓ Do you miss deadlines?

✓ Do you wait to work on projects until the last minute?

✓ Does it take you longer than two minutes to find a file?

✓ Is your living or workspace so cluttered with "stuff" that you need to add an extension on to the house?

✓ Do you have trouble finding a place to work in your cubicle?

✓ Do you have an obstacle course of toys in your living room or den?

✓ Are you running out of closet and drawer space?

✓ Do you find yourself staring into the closet and you haven't a clue as to what you are looking at?

✓ Are there items in your refrigerator that are totally unrecognizable?

✓ Are you habitually late for appointments?

✓ Do you forget to attend meetings and events because you forgot to list them on your calendar?

✓ Is your dining room table so cluttered that your junk mail serves as placemats and entertaining has become embarrassing?

✓ Do you search endlessly for a computer file because you forgot the name?

✓ Do you have a problem throwing "stuff" away?

✓ Do you find there is no time to enjoy the things that are most important to you?

If you answered yes to any of these questions, welcome to the I Hate Filing Club. Just as I have helped thousands of people over the past two decades, I'll help you find organization, sanity and ultimately empowerment.

How Can the I Hate Filing Club Help?

The I Hate Filing Club was originally created in 1986 for office professionals who hated filing. After a survey of the organizationally challenged (that's most people you know), we discovered filing was the most dreaded task. We all know we can't make it go away, but we also know it can be easier. Filing seems to be the perfect metaphor for the things we don't want to do, or don't know how to make easier through easy organizational steps. When we waste energy dreading something, it ultimately becomes more complicated and draining. So here's how I'd like you to think of filing when you read this book: however large or small, if you dread doing it, it has power over you. Whether it's filing, cleaning your kitchen, folding your clothes, paying your bills, or making time for your family or friends, if you don't feel organized and in control, you are losing valuable time and energy. You reclaim power, and become empowered, when you just get it done and take action. Here's the secret—if you follow my advice, you don't have to hate filing! With this premise, the I Hate Filing Club was founded and in turn it found people who thrived on this advice.

By 1995, the club had over ninety-five thousand members, people desperately seeking solutions as to how to organize not just their professional lives but their personal lives as well. Today the I Hate Filing Club helps members with not only filing but with organizational solutions for all aspects of their lives. The club continues to gain new members from all walks of life seeking less hectic lives. Most of us struggle to balance our lives. There are so many homes with two working parents and many with only one parent. Keeping our lives together becomes increasingly more difficult. I have discovered in my work that today's lifestyle cries out for organization, and the club strives to help its members achieve that with monthly newsletters and a Web site filled with solutions. For the past eight years, I've enjoyed serving as president and helping people achieve their organizational goals. Simply put, organization changed my life and I know it can change yours.

Apply Organization to Three Areas of Your Life

Most people think of organization as just clearing and cleaning up clutter. Now this may be true, but there are many other aspects that need to be considered in order for you to improve the quality of your life. Some people are innately more organized just by the nature of who they are and others seem to need that push and be given the tools to help them achieve organizational bliss.

 ### The Mind

First let's talk about your *mind*. Think of it as your personal filing cabinet storing all of your ideas, tasks and responsibilities. Your mind is what you use to collect all of the data that you are bombarded with daily and how you sort it out. The more organized you are with your thoughts, the easier it is to take on challenges. In this book we will talk about ways to organize your thoughts, like writing down goals, using your daily planner, and keeping your mind clear of clutter and open for challenges and ideas.

The Body

Your *body* is the way that you present yourself to the world. According to communication experts, people form opinions within the first seven seconds of meeting you. They spend the next ten minutes trying to confirm their original perceptions. We have all been there. At one time or another we have all said, "There's something about that person that bugs me." Or "They really have it together." Your look and your body language play a major role in your communication success. Take a moment before you leave the house and look in the mirror, practice your body language. Think about the image you want to convey not only to others but to yourself as well.

Physical Space

Your *physical space* is what surrounds you and the space in which you live, work, breathe and interact with others. You may consider your space to be your desk, cubicle, office, closet or the kitchen counter. These are the places in your life where you live, eat and breathe. Clutter keeps you from being productive and causes stress. Set a schedule to clean up and stick to it. It only takes twenty-seven days to create a habit. When these three areas of your life are all in sync, stress and anxiety will be but just a memory, allowing peace and harmony into your life.

 ## Write It Down

When I was younger, I never felt strongly one way or the other about organization. My life was haphazard and pretty much "as you go." Being a single mother with an infant child makes you look at life and your daily routine in a whole different light. I can remember sitting at my kitchen table looking over my options. I knew I had to get my act together if I was going to make my life work.

I needed to balance my work and home life, keep the house neat, and, most important, spend quality time with my son, Marc. I wrote down my goals and a strict routine was set that would allow me to achieve them.

So at this point, I ask that you put your ideas and goals in writing so they become visible and you know what you need to do. Now I know you've heard this before, others have offered this advice as well, but I have to tell you that it really, really works. When you write your goals down, they become real and success becomes more reachable. This is something we will explore further in the book. It's important to write down goals, short term and long term. Your short-term goals should be the steps you need to take to achieve the ultimate goal.

Take a few minutes to write down goals for yourself. What do you want to achieve in a week, a month and a year? What do you want to get from this book? Later in the book, we will come back and take a look at your goals.

ACT

First things first, it's time for you to get your "ACT" together. ACT is my philosophy of organization. A = take *action,* C = *clear or clean* and T = *toss.*

However, as good as the routine might be, when you have one of those "life happens" moments, you need to step back, take a deep breath and remind yourself, *I have to get my ACT together.* I remember when my son was about three, I had a job that paid an incentive for being on time. One day I needed to get my son to his grandmother's and myself to work and I could not find my keys. My first reaction was to panic. I looked for the keys in all of the usual places without success. Okay, I took a deep breath. I remembered that Marc loved to play with my keys, and all I had to do was think, *If I were three, what would I do with the keys?* Because we had established a routine to clean up his toys before bedtime, my instinct was to go to the toy chest. Success, keys found, and on time to work. Lesson learned! If I had not taken the time to organize my thought process, I would not have known where they were. An established routine combined with keeping a clear head was the recipe for success. Being organized can play a significant role in relieving stress, increasing your well-being and giving you time to do the things that are most important to you. For many that includes being with family, time to enjoy your favorite pastime or just time to relax.

So What Does It Mean to Get Your ACT Together?

You will find that I refer to this philosophy many times in the book. It is a cornerstone of how we can change our lives for the better. It relates to three steps, taking Action, Clearing or Cleaning or Tossing, and becoming aware of your own personal workspace and what that means to you. Your workspace could be your desk at work or your home office, your kitchen, a hobby area, or it can be any room in your home. It's the place you call "your space." And it's time to take control.

Let's take a look at these three areas:

1. **Taking "Action."** This could involve opening mail, having a project come across your desk, or receiving an invitation. When you take action, you respond immediately so that tasks aren't overlooked or become overwhelming. Here are a few tips for taking action.

   Opening mail: always open your mail near a trash can, so you eliminate junk mail immediately; have a sorter for items that need to be followed up at a later date and create a file for bills to be paid. The file should hold everything you need to pay your bills along with a bill payment schedule. Whether it's junk mail or a problem at work, don't let it become an issue or sit around.

Projects: be sure to plan any tasks or projects with a defined timeline. For example, taxes: Every January you should set up a folder for taxes. Sort papers as you go so you will have everything you need when it comes time to file.

2. **Clean or Clear.** I always suggest tidying up at the end of the day. Picture arriving at work and having your desk ready to go, or not falling over toys or clothes in the middle of the night or morning at home. File away completed tasks, color code and label active files, mark your calendar or diary with to-do items for the next day and code them according to priority. Enlist the family to help; with kids, you can make it a game that they will enjoy.

3. **Toss.** This is probably the most difficult for people. We all hate letting go, whether it be materially or emotionally. You always think it will come in handy one day. Before you know it you have a room filled with items that may come in handy . . . one day. Here is a good rule of thumb: If you haven't worn it or used it in two years, it's probably time to toss it or donate it. Purge paper files every six months. Toss any files you no longer need and store the needed papers in an archive file.

Become a master at organization and control all that surrounds you. The following chapters offer some great solutions and tips on keeping yourself and your workspace, wherever that may be, organized and free from clutter.

CHAPTER 2

ORGANIZING YOUR WORKSPACE

Wherever Your "Workspace" May Be

On a Monday morning, Sally (last name omitted to protect the sloppy) sat down at her desk and looked for her scissors. The last time she'd seen them was three months ago. In front of her lay reams of loose papers and reports, a couple of opened Life Savers rolls, a half-eaten Clark Bar, a hat that she didn't recognize, a menu she'd cut out from the newspaper, some bills she'd been paying, a couple of notes she had written to herself to remind her to clean up her desk, and there were several memos she piled on her desk that had been there over the last few days, weeks and months. *Funny,* she thought to herself, *I know those scissors are here somewhere.*

She simply gave up looking for them on Wednesday. *Somebody probably stole them,* she said to herself. On Thursday she borrowed another pair of scissors from a co-worker. The co-worker volunteered to also give Sally a book of matches so that she could burn the mess that had become her desk. Sally wanted to be angry at this co-worker, whom she hadn't really liked since the time the co-worker had refused to chip in $1.00 for a cake they were going to get for someone who was leaving the company. That was two years ago, but Sally never got rid of anything—especially a grudge! Anyway, Sally took the scissors from the co-worker, passed on the matches and at that moment swore that she'd clean up her desk and get the mess put away so that she'd no longer bear the brunt of intra-office jokes about her disorganization. She decided she was going to do it this time, once and for all . . .

Right after lunch.

If you're like Sally and tens of millions of other people, you spend a huge percentage of your time—and your energy—digging out, through, under and around piles of clutter. Clutter, in some strange, bizarre way has become your "companion." (With friends like these you don't need enemies!) But it doesn't have to be that way. Having an organized desk and workspace can save you time, increase your productivity, and give you some semblance of order in your life and a welcome rest from the nagging feeling that things have somehow gotten, shall we say, a bit out of control. Maybe your sanity somehow hangs in the balance. Maybe this is a change you have been putting off for so long you've just about thrown up your hands and accepted your life as it is. Don't give up. Dump your old, stale Clark Bars, pull together all of your loose desk papers and vow to see the bottom of your desk no matter what happens. It's time to get on the road to *organization*! To do this, there are some very easy solutions. All you have to do is follow the suggestions in the following chapters! Ready, okay, here goes!

Desktop Distractions?

Six tips for keeping your desk organized and yourself more productive.

Psst . . . Is there somebody in there? Is that you behind that monstrous assortment of "stuff" cluttering your desk or space? Most people don't even realize it, but a disorganized desk can cause tremendous frustration—and lost productivity that can mean having to stay late at the office or lose valuable time trying to find things that have simply disappeared!

I remember someone once telling me a story about a lost file that was blamed on everyone in her department; everyone, that is, but her. Several months later, when new desks were delivered and she had to remove the clutter from her old desk, guess what she found? Yep, the lost file. Fact is, a messy desk makes it extremely difficult to go about your daily routine.

The following are six practical suggestions for avoiding desktop distractions:

1. **File immediately. Do it NOW!** In other words, "avoid pile-ups!" I know it can be difficult to keep up with your

filing when you get really busy, but to keep your desk neat and orderly, it's imperative that you don't allow paper-work to grow into unmanageable stacks. Keep active files on your desk in color-coded folders.

2. **Use the tops of credenzas and lateral file cabinets.** These pieces of organizing furniture can be found in almost every office. And even if you work in a cubicle, there's probably a flat-top credenza or cabinet nearby, providing space where you can store such things as binders and cat-alogs rather than letting them clutter your desktop.

3. **Utilize shelves.** This is another smart location for storing things that might otherwise cause confusion by taking up space on your desk. A shelf, not your desk, is the proper place for items such as phone books, magazines and videos.

4. **Create "drop spots."** Perhaps a wall organizer, or some other kind of receptacle to temporarily drop memos, notes and other small papers, keeping those kinds of easy-to-lose documents off your desk until you have time to look at them.

5. **Try not to get too personal.** Minimize the urge to clutter your desk with an excessive amount of personal items, such as photographs and knickknacks, etc. It's a good idea to have some personal items, this establishes a commit-ment to your space. That picture of your wife or husband is nice, and those kids and grandchildren are adorable, but a whole family album (especially if it's not your

family) is a bit much, don't you think? Of course, it's great to have some remembrances of your loved ones in your workspace, just don't overdo it so that your desk is covered with them. Also, knickknacks have their place, but making your desk look like a thrift store counter is well . . . counterproductive!

6. **Accessorize.** Office organizers, such as file sorters with different compartments, and plastic bins that can hold almost anything, are ideal for storing a wide array of office materials that might instead accumulate on your desk. Use these accessories for things such as folders, letters and CDs.

Dear Sharon:

I feel so unorganized in my office filing, i.e., keeping track of files in the cabinet not being used and keeping track of files I am using that I need for a project. Do you have any suggestions on how I might file or keep my files? In other words, I run out of time filing what needs to be filed, and I find myself searching for files that I have in a pile by my desk because I need them for projects I'm currently working on! Any suggestions? Thanks!

Deborah, Administrative Assistant

Dear Deborah,

Wow, it seems that nothing is going right in your filing life. First of all, files that are no longer used should be put into what is called an "archive" file. This could be a separate cabinet or just a section of one drawer, depending on how much archive material you have. The point is to take files that are no longer active and get them out of the way (but not thrown away in case you need them). As for searching for files that are piled on your desk, you should only have active files on your desk. Keep them labeled and in color-coded clear folders for easy reference. All other files should be filed away. A great way to keep up is to devote five to ten minutes at the end of each day to filing.

Correspondence Course

Got huge piles of incoming/outgoing mail? Here are fast ways to organize it.

It's a constant challenge faced by all of us who work in offices and at home—how to efficiently manage the continual stream of envelopes, letters and other correspondence that seems to pile up each and every day.

Not to worry, I have a four-step approach that will give you

 ideas about how to handle the flow of mail in your workspace and how to avoid dreaded "pile syndrome" that can bury your desk and rob you of productivity. Earlier I gave a few tips on managing mail. To avoid pile-ups, try these tips.

First, get yourself four stackable in/out trays or a sorter for your desk or wall. Then, label and utilize each of the trays or sections of the sorter into the following categories: "Things to Do"; "Items for Routing"; "Items to Read"; and "Items to File."

As soon as possible after office mail arrives at your desk, sort it into each of the above categories and place the material in its respective place. "Things to Do" might, for example, involve mail you have received that requires a response. "Items for Routing" would include materials that have to be forwarded to other people in your office or throughout your company. "Items to Read" could be simply non-priority letters or other correspondence that you will want to read eventually but don't need to do right away. "Items to File" will probably become a kind of catch-all for much of the mail that arrives at your desk—this material will be transferred from your workspace to a file cabinet. However, do not let it sit for too long in your "Items to File" tray because the amount of material in the tray will build up quickly. Try to ACT on each item as soon as possible.

The above techniques are straightforward and simple to implement in your business office and also at home, whether it's in an actual home office or just on the corner of a table you use to collect your mail. Try these techniques for yourself. I'm sure you'll be able to organize your correspondence much easier than if you had to deal with piles that are not only messy, but can also cause items to get lost.

If all else fails, and you simply can't get your ACT (take Action, Clear or Toss) together . . . well, you can always borrow a book of matches . . . or use your own (if you can find them!).

Dear Sharon:

This is more of a personal question than business related. I was wondering if you have any suggestions/tips for filing and organizing incoming mail and bills at home? Also, do you know how long you should keep your files at home?

Lori, Administrative Assistant

Clearing Clutter 101

A fast course for the fast track.

If you're sitting in the office, at home or at your workspace right now, look around you. Are there little piles of paper with no

Dear Lori,

You would be amazed how many questions we get about filing at home, and it's no wonder, because everybody seems to have some kind of "home office" these days. For incoming mail I always suggest file as you go. Sort mail and immediately throw away junk mail. Here are some tips on what files to keep from a national title company: birth/death certificates, marriage/divorce papers, wills and passports should be kept indefinitely (store originals in a fire-proof box or safety deposit box). Keep tax papers seven years, insurance policies four years after the expiration date, mortgage papers four years after making the last payment, home improvement receipts as long as you own the house and credit card bills three years (if your credit card company sends a year-end statement that should be sufficient). Keep warranties and manuals for as long as you own the product. I would keep birthday cards for as long as you think someone might ask to see them.

home? Are there pens and pencils sitting in the corners of your desk? Does your in-box over-floweth? Are there toys or clothes that have not been put away? This is clutter—the little things from your daily life that, up to now, rarely had a place to "live."

According to researchers, higher amounts of clutter can actually contribute to a higher level of stress in your life. As well, psychological studies have shown that organizing your home can make a very positive difference in the way you feel about your surroundings and your life in general. So let's look at containing the clutter. The following are a few tips to help you get ahead of the game and lower that stress!

The first thing to do is find a place for your things. If you've already done this, congratulations and move on to the next tip. If not, welcome to the beginning of a clutter-free life. I'm going to repeat a few tips from the first chapter; I can't stress enough how these simple rules can help ease the clutter in your daily life.

1. Take a good look at what the top three to five clutter problems are. Paper? Magazines? Pens, pencils, paper clips? Other stuff? Once you've identified them, think of the ideal place where they should "live." These places should be easy to get to, but out of your main workspace and line of sight. For example, pens and other office instruments should be kept in a drawer or container. It's easy to get to and out of sight. Use a labeling tool to label the inside top of the drawer "Office Tools." This will reinforce your mind to remember where to put things.

2. Do the same with the other clutter piles. Paper should be sorted into folders based on priority. The simplest way is to use color file folders to color code your filing categories. For example, use red for "Important," blue for "Active," and green for "To File." Put a label on the top to remember it, too. This way, there's always a home for the clutter on your desk. When using active files that need to be on your desk or accessible, color coding is the best

solution. Experts say that color coding helps you find files 50 percent faster. You may want to consider using a desktop or wall hanging sorter for filing solutions.

3. Take five minutes every day before you leave work to make sure that all the "little" stuff is put away. This means putting pens, pencils and other instruments in the places you've designated. You won't believe how nice it is to come back to a clean and inviting workspace. Apply the same rule to your home each night. Be sure all toys and clothing are stored in their proper places.

4. Items like the daily mail and newspapers can soon turn into piles that remain for weeks. Use the tips I gave you for prioritizing your mail. Buy a simple letter sorter and, using a labelmaker, label the compartments "Bills," "Letters, "To Look At." Anything else should be junk and tossed right away, but remember, if it's a credit card application or other mail piece with personal info on it, a shredder will pretty much guarantee that no one can use that mail for illegal purposes.

5. Children are great, full of life and a joy to be around. Unfortunately, they also are some of the largest creators of clutter! Even though they're young, children can be affected by clutter too. Help them create a system where all their stuff can be stored. Color bins that are labeled not only help them put stuff away, but you can also make a game out of it so that it becomes fun and a learning experience.

6. The same goes for the kids' clothes drawers. Label the

inside top of the drawers with the contents. This will help them be a part of the solution, not the problem, by letting them put their own clothes away. Plus, it helps out a lot around the house.

7. Try organizing your closet. Consider hanging your clothes by type and color. Organize your shoes in cubbies or a hanging shoe rack. If you keep your shoes in boxes, consider labeling them with a picture. The best part about my closet being organized this way is that I can count on fifteen minutes more of sleep every morning.

Hopefully these few tips can help get you ahead of the clutter at home. The first thing to remember in controlling the clutter is commitment.

Dear Sharon,

Has anyone come up with a "Rules for Filing" protocol? For example, I have three kids. When one of them sees the doctor and gets a receipt, should I file it in a Family Health file, the child's file or the insurance company file? I am having a hard time deciding what file heading to set up. Thanks for your help.

Kevin

Dear Kevin,

Sounds like you are in need of some filing assistance in the home office. Although I know of no actual "rules for filing" etiquette as you mention, I do recommend filing by subject. The first thing you should do is to think about what you need to keep and then make a list. The items on this list will be your subjects. No one product that I can recommend is versatile enough that it eases the pain of organizing the many different kinds of family-related paperwork that accumulates every month in the average household. Folders come in different colors for fast retrieval. You may want to create sub-categories in your folders, for example, "Medical" can be the main subject and the interior folders can be used for each person in the family.

Spring Cleaning

When flowers are blooming, it's the perfect time to weed out clutter. Here are five quick tips.

Each year, we celebrate spring. It is a time for renewal. As the spring season rolls around each year, it's a great time to spruce-up your office and clean out the tons of papers, notes, reports and other miscellaneous items that have accumulated over the winter.

Use this time to also clean out your closets.

To help make it easier for you to get your office freshened up so you can be more productive as summer approaches, here are five straightforward ideas about the best and perhaps most important places to begin your spring cleaning chores.

1. **Your desk.** This is probably where you spend most of your day. As a result, it's imperative that you keep it free of clutter. Be sure to remove any piles of papers and carefully file them in their appropriate folders in your file cabinet. For projects you're currently working on, try using a multi-section project folder such as the Pendaflex® Hanging Vertical File or Project Sorter. This versatile color-coded system allows you to collect project records as you gather them and still keep them at hand.

2. **Your files.** Go into the file drawer right now and chances are you'll see papers that are old and outdated. Create a separate archive file for these documents, and put all your archive files into their own section of your filing system. This will keep the "live" section of the system less crowded so you can look up current paperwork faster. If you can, remove old files and put them in a storage bin.

3. **Your shelves.** It's likely that some overflow of the stuff that would have ended up on your desk, eventually found its way to your shelves. File away any loose documents on the shelves, before they get lost. Remove old, outdated

magazines. And organize any books or binders you may have on the shelves by using bookends to make certain the books and binders stand up straight and are neatly arranged for quick referencing.

4. **Your computer.** Back out digital files you're no longer working on and save them from your hard drive onto external media such as CDs and DVDs. Excessive clutter residing on your hard drive can dramatically slow down computer performance.

5. **Your business contacts organizer.** Whether you're using a standard card file or an electronic name/address organizer, you should use spring as an occasion to go in and remove the names of people you no longer do business with (you may not want to throw away old contacts, but at least take them out of the active organizer for more overall efficiency).

Vacation Planner

Leaving on your summer getaway? Put this quick plan in place first, then relax!

Each year, when the holidays or summer finally arrives, your thoughts probably turn to your vacation. Obviously, you want to be able to leave all the stresses of the office behind you without having to worry about how the office is getting along without you

while you're gone. You also want to make sure your home is secure.

What's more, you also want to be able to return to an office that has not become complete chaos in your absence. And perhaps most importantly, you definitely don't want to get a phone call while you're away because a co-worker cannot find a document in the file, or has some other question that only you can answer.

Here are some practical tips for planning your getaway so that it can be truly relaxing:

1. **Buddy up.** Before embarking on your vacation, ask a co-worker to act as the "invisible you" while you're gone. Chances are, they won't have to do much more than maybe reach into your file drawer to pull a document once in a while. The point is, someone can be there to intercept any problems while you're enjoying your vacation. Offer to act as the "buddy" for your co-worker when

   he or she goes away, and both of you will benefit. At home, let your neighbor know you'll be away. This can alert them to any suspicious activity.

2. **Leave notes.** If you're in the middle of an important project when your vacation arrives, leave behind a "status report" that explains what has been completed on the project and what the next steps will be. This will show your boss that you're on top of everything, while also helping to answer any questions while you're not there.

3. **Point the way.** The day prior to your vacation, create a list of instructions where co-workers can find current project documents in the file. It's likely that someone will have to reference something while you're soaking up the summer sun. Have the post office hold your mail. A full mailbox is a clear sign that you're away.

4. **Clear the clutter.** Before you go away, clean your desk of all loose paperwork to help prevent important papers from getting lost.

5. **Designate a "drop spot."** Place a desktop tray or receptacle in the middle of your desk before leaving for your vacation and explain to co-workers (including mail-room personnel) that this is where you want correspondence to be put while you're gone. You might also consider using a desktop file for this purpose. This will keep your work area organized so you won't return to a chaotic desk topped with piles of messy papers, memos and phone message slips.

6. **Back up all digital files.** You should do this anyway, at least every week if not every day. However, it's especially important to copy computer files from your hard drive to external media (CDs, etc.) before you leave for vacation. You never know, a storm could come along while you're thousands of miles away, wiping out weeks of work that you thought was safely saved.

Welcome Back

It's time to get back into the swing of things.

It was wonderful, the annual family getaway. Perhaps you went to the shore, or a theme park, or that special hideaway in the mountains. Now, you're back and your desk is a disaster—stacked to the ceiling with all the correspondence that accumulated while you were gone. Before you start pulling your hair out and contemplating how you'll ever get through it all and actually find your desk again, try these three simple approaches:

1. **Sort things out.** Instead of just haphazardly grabbing every memo, letter and other piece of paper then deciding where each goes, first separate the memos into their own neatly arranged stack. Do the same with the letters and everything else. Once you've sorted everything into its own category of paperwork, you'll see that it's much easier to then begin deciding what to Act on, what to Clear and file and what to Toss. A good way to remember these three steps is getting your ACT together. You will see that I refer to this often in the book.

2. **Identify your priorities.** Obviously, some of the paperwork that piled up on your desk while you were away on vacation is "hotter" than others and requires more immediate attention from you. Yet, you'd be surprised how many people are

simply overwhelmed by the amount of papers they need to go through and forget a fundamental objective of being well organized: Decide, based on the dates the documents arrived at your desk and the importance of the people and projects associated with those papers, which you should address first and then do so. You might be amazed how prioritizing, as basic as it sounds, can help make even the most intimidating mountains of papers disappear more quickly. Try sorting the items that are hotter in a red folder.

3. **Resist the "moving pile" syndrome.** It can be very tempting to simply transfer the stacks of paper on your desk to another spot in your work area, perhaps a credenza or maybe even the floor. Sure, you'll be busy when you return from vacation and there will be lots of responsibilities you need to attend to right away—however, simply moving piles of papers from one place to another accomplishes nothing in the long run. You'll still have to file (Act or Toss) those memos, letters and other documents eventually. So why not do it now and clear your desk right away, allowing you to work most productively as soon as possible? Try never handling a piece of paper twice.

4. **Manage your active files.** There are times when you want to keep some active files at hand. Pendaflex came out with a great line of products for pilers called PileSmart.

Try using color-coded folders. According to a study by *The Wall Street Journal,* color coding can help you find files 50 percent faster. Try to avoid those piles of paper with rubber bands.

Dear Sharon:

How do you make someone tidy when you are not tidy yourself?

Carol, Training & Development Specialist

Dear Carol,

This is a tough question, Carol, but a good one. You could of course dump everything on the top of your desk into a bin and shove it into the closet each night before you leave work. This way you will create the illusion that you are tidy, or, because you may not be able to lead by example, you should lead by suggesting situations that include a cause and an effect. For instance, explain to the person that if they file just once a week, files will tend to build up and be harder to organize. However, if they file every day, the job will be easier and the files themselves will be more efficient. Another example would be to point out that misplacing things on a desk could be caused by too much clutter. Demonstrate to the person that if they clean their desk periodically, the effect will be that things will not get lost in the mess. This could be an opportunity for you to get yourself organized as well.

Think of it as a win-win.

CHAPTER 3

FILING TIME-SAVERS

A Place for Everything

All right, you know you put that file somewhere. You're not sure when you last saw it so you try to retrace your steps. Did I leave it somewhere, is it misfiled? Sound familiar?

One of the greatest time-stealers in corporate offices as well as households involves the inability to file and organize in the most efficient way possible. Most of my Ask Sharon questions are about this category. One of the most important tips I can offer you is to never handle a piece of paper twice. When retrieving or opening a document you really only have three choices. Act, Clear and Toss. I think of it as getting and keeping your ACT together. (There it is again. Do you think I am trying to tell you something?) Drawing upon many years of experience in organization and filing, here are some great tips for setting up and maintaining a filing system. You will find that I refer to color coding and labeling often. These are two tips that I find extremely valuable.

Missing in Action

Surefire ways to locate a missing document.

I know it can be frustrating beyond belief; your boss has asked you to find the list of regional sales territories you photocopied just a few weeks ago. Unfortunately, it's nowhere to be found. You're sure you filed it, but you're having no luck at all in your search.

Before you go into a free-fall panic, try these twelve proven tips for locating the "lost" document (compiled from the official Pendaflex® "How to File" Guide):

1. **Start at your desktop.** Although I constantly (and strongly) suggest that people not allow piles of paper to accumulate on their desks, many times it's very hard to avoid a messy workspace—especially when you're extra busy and working with many active files. A desktop filled with stacks of records as well as many loose papers scattered around is a perfect hiding spot for a missing document. Carefully check under and around each pile and beneath each loose paper.

2. **Recheck the folder where the paper should be.** You might have skipped over individual papers. Go through

the entire file slowly.

3. **Go to your in/out box.** Maybe you mistakenly placed the  document in that tray on the corner of your desk, the tray that's normally reserved for ingoing and outgoing mail. Take a look, you might find it there.

4. **Check the folders directly in front and in back of the folder where the paper should be.** The paper might have mistakenly been put into a neighboring folder.

5. **Look between the folders.** Sometimes you think you've put a paper inside the folder, but you've actually missed.

6. **Double-check the subject name of the paper you're looking for.** Perhaps you're searching for the sales "Territory" list, but maybe you accidentally filed the document in the sales "Results" folder.

7. **Check the "pending" trays of other employees.** It's possible that someone else is holding the paper for some reason. Also check your co-workers' in and out trays.

8. **Think who else may have needed the document.** Maybe someone pulled the sales territory list and didn't tell you. Use a process of elimination to narrow down the people who might have borrowed the document.

9. **Check the wastebasket.** You never know. The paper could have been thrown out by mistake.

10. **Backtrack your steps.** You may have left it at someone's desk or even at the copy machine.

11. **Check office machinery.** Perhaps the document, without your knowledge, has been brought by a co-worker to a fax machine or copy machine. Take a look, you may just find it there.

12. **Make a call to the mail room.** Many companies employ mail-room workers who are continuously "making the rounds" throughout offices, delivering incoming mail as well as picking up outgoing mail. Maybe your document was mistakenly identified by a mail-room employee as "outgoing" and the document is sitting either in the mail cart or in the mail room itself.

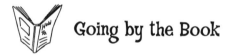 Going by the Book

How to create a filing manual that makes your record-keeping system more productive.

So, your filing system is working pretty well. You've got all your records arranged in neat alphabetical order. And you've got numerical subsections that break the system down into more manageable parts.

You understand your files inside and out, but what if someone new came to work in your office? Would they also understand how your filing system works? Do you have the time to spend explaining your filing procedures to them?

One of the best ways to ensure that your recordkeeping system is easy for everyone to understand is to create your own manual that can serve as a guide for utilizing the system most efficiently. The manual doesn't have to be fancy; it can be typed or even handwritten and put into a ring binder or simply stapled together. The important thing is, it will provide a "blueprint" for the way the system works so that everyone can file and find papers quickly.

Here's what your manual should explain:

- ✓ How your files are arranged: By name? By subject? Alphabetically? Numerically? A combination of alphabetical and numerical subdivisions?
- ✓ Where the file cabinets are and what each drawer contains.
- ✓ The ways in which you have color coded your files and what each color represents.
- ✓ Any rules you would like everyone to follow, such as the need to "sign-out" files whenever they're removed.
- ✓ How to transfer active files to "inactive" or "archive" storage.
- ✓ A brief index, continually updated, that shows at a glance all the different categories that are in your filing system and in what drawer(s) they can be found.

Creating a filing manual will probably only take you an hour or less. And trust me, it's time well spent. Keeping a continually up-to-date manual that clearly explains your filing system can save you lots of time in the long run by helping to avoid lost files and reducing recordkeeping confusion.

In Working Order

Ways to help ensure that your file system operates most efficiently.

You've probably heard the phrase, "The more things change, the more they stay the same." Well, that axiom certainly holds true for your files. If your company is like most, its filing needs are constantly changing as the company grows. For example, new filing categories need to be added as your company's markets expand, as its customer lists widen and as new products or services are added. The good news is, the rules for efficient trouble-free filing will still apply, no matter how many changes your company or department goes through.

Did you know that by filing and finding papers faster, your company could actually save tens of thousands of dollars every year? It's true. Searching through a messy, inefficient filing system is very unproductive and costs businesses big money in time that could be put to better use.

Try these suggestions, and you'll be amazed by how much neater and better organized your files will become—and how much quicker everyone in your office will be able to find the records they want.

1. **Use hanging and interior folders.** As opposed to standard file folders, hanging folders do what their name implies: they hang on rails and glide inside your file drawer.

   Interior folders *are* designed to fit inside the hanging folders, allowing you to subdivide related papers into individual categories within an overall hanging folder category.

2. **Use labelmakers to create custom labels.** By utilizing an electronic labelmaker to print self-stick labels, you'll be sure to create file headings that are always legible, preventing misfiles. Plus, you'll be able to create your labels using different size fonts, colors and other special effects to make individual filing categories stand out.

3. **Use color.** By filing with colored folders, instead of just plain manila ones, you can actually improve filing speed by 33 percent or more!

4. **Use patience.** Above all, keep your cool, even if papers in your file sometimes become misplaced. According to recordkeeping studies, more than 90 percent of the time when people think that a document has been lost, it's actually just been misfiled somewhere in the file drawer—so don't panic.

5. **Repair torn pages.** Ripped, tattered documents do not sit properly inside file folders, tending to ride up in the folder and obscure the filing tabs. Use transparent tape to fix the rips before inserting a torn document into your file.

6. **Staple related papers together.** This will allow you to access a whole bunch of papers dealing with the same subject, all at the same time.

7. **File regularly.** If you let "to be filed" papers build up, the task will become more insurmountable as the days and weeks pass by.

8. **Don't let papers sit on desks and credenzas.** This is a sure way to lose something. Check every day to make certain that important documents are not left out in the open.

9. **Use "out" guides.** These are cards that are placed into your file to signal when a folder has been removed from the file. Blank spaces on the card allow the person to enter their name and the date the file was taken, making it easy to keep track of circulating records.

10. **Limit borrowing time.** Check your out guides at least once a week, and if a file has not been returned, follow up with the person who took it, helping to reduce the chance of a lost file.

Get the Hang of It, Quickly

Reasons why hanging filing is the fastest filing.

Now that we have discussed how to keep your filing system running smoothly, let's talk about why hanging folders and interior folders work best.

1. **Neatness counts.** In a busy office, paperwork builds continuously, and if the files are sloppy it can take you much longer to find something. Non-hanging folders tend to sag or slump to the bottom of the filing drawer, making your filing system unsightly and difficult to deal with. Because they're suspended on rails, hanging folders will not sag or slump, ensuring the neatest, most efficient approach to filing.

2. **Always a full view.** With hanging filing, tabs always stay upright and perfectly aligned, providing a clear and complete view of file headings for at-a-glance referencing.

3. **The advantages of gliding.** Hanging folders have built-in hooks specially designed to glide freely on drawer rails. This allows for fast, "fingertip" access to individual records.

4. **Versatility personified.** Pendaflex hanging filing products are the world's most versatile performers, available  in many different styles to complete your hanging system, including: Extra Capacity Folders for organizing thick items such as catalogs and reports; Hanging CD File for storing computer media; Hanging Expandable Files for growing projects, Hanging Partition Folders with built-in dividers, and many other styles.

Almost everyone is familiar with the old line that says "divide and conquer" and it certainly applies to filing. Fact is, breaking your files up into smaller categories is one of the best ways to file and find papers more easily, more accurately and, perhaps most important, more quickly!

Among the simplest and most effective methods for dividing your files into subsections is to use what are called "interior folders." As their name implies, interior folders are specially designed to fit inside of hanging folders and you use them to divide related records in each hanging folder for faster look-ups.

For example, perhaps you have a hanging folder with the subject heading "Customer Purchase Orders." Inside the hanging folder, you could put several interior folders, each containing a separate set of purchase orders for that customer. This will allow you to reach into the hanging folder and instantly access just the records you need for a particular customer. Another great thing about interior folders is that they can be color coded within your hanging filing system for the most filing efficiency. Still another advantage of using interior folders is that they allow you to go to the filing drawer, and remove just the records you need, leaving the hanging folder in the cabinet to help extend folder life. In addition, removing interior folders makes it simple and convenient to take records from the file to your desk, where you can reference the material you want more easily. Want to make all your filing go faster and smoother? Be sure to use interior folders to subdivide records inside your hanging folders!

The Color of Money

How you or your company can save big by filing more efficiently with color coding.

You've heard the expression "Time is money" and, as I've said, nowhere is it more true than in a business or home office. The

 fact is, just about any business can save tons of money by reducing the time it takes to perform certain tasks—particularly repetitive tasks such as filing. And one of the best ways to speed filing time is by using colored file folders versus non-colored (manila) folders (I like to refer to them as vanilla folders—no flavor or imagination).

Studies by recordkeeping experts have proven that color in a filing system can actually decrease the amount of time it takes to find a file by as much as 50 percent! Now let's look at that in dollar amounts. Say, for example, that a person working in an average office is making $15 per hour and that person spends seven hours per week filing with non-colored folders. That adds up to a total of $105. But if they used colored folders and cut their filing time in half, it might only cost their company $52.50 to get the filing completed. Of course, there's another part to this equation—productivity. If the person in the example were to spend less time on filing, they could spend more time on other business projects.

Now you may ask, exactly how does color coding make filing

faster and more efficient? Well let's say you assign all your personnel files to red folders, all your customer files to green folders, and all your follow-up files to blue folders. Then, the next time you go to the filing drawer for a personnel file, you can just look in the "red" section instead of having to plow through all the folders. Other ideas for color coding include breaking down your files by days of the week or months of the year and designating a different colored folder for each day or month. The color-coding possibilities are actually limitless, depending on how your business is run, along with your individual recordkeeping needs.

The bottom line is, utilizing color in your filing system will indeed save you time, which in turn will save your company money. And that can make you look very good when it's time for your annual review and pay raise! Try organizing your files in blocks of color and see for yourself how much easier, faster and less frustrating it is to locate the exact file you want every time you go into the filing drawer!

Colorful Ideas

Twenty possibilities for color coding your files to enhance office efficiency.

In the business office, you could color code your files according to

1. Project
2. Days of the week

3. Months

4. Year

5. Department

6. Customers/key accounts

7. Confidentiality of the filed material

8. Priority

9. Fiscal period

10. People on your team/responsibilities of team members

In your home office, you could color code files containing

1. Insurance papers

2. Tax records

3. Receipts

4. Medical records

5. Mortgage payments

6. Automobile maintenance records

7. Bank statements

8. Warranties

9. Utility bills

10. Charitable contributions

Dear Sharon:

Why do they make hanging folders with colored tabs? In my opinion, it is too difficult to read the words through the yellow, red, purple, etc. tabs. Am I the only one who feels this way? I say stick to clear tabs; it would make my job much easier.

Janet, Office Manager/Bookkeeper

Dear Janet,

While we're glad to see you're using color hanging folders to keep your files neat, I do get a few negative comments about colored indexing tabs, mostly about the darker colors. Colored tabs are designed to match the colors of the folders themselves, creating uniformity within the filing system. By assigning colored tabs to entire filing categories, you create blocks of color in the file drawer, which separates categories into quickly identifiable sections for instant finding. As for your difficulty in reading words through colored tabs, I suggest using an electronic labelmaker to print your tab headings and using the label on the outside of the tab. This way you still maintain a color-coded system and the labels are visible. DYMO® labelers, for instance, make it easy to print bold letters that are sure to be easily legible through your colored tabs or over them.

The following articles deal with setting up your filing system from scratch and what works best for you.

Something from Nothing

Seven simple steps for starting an easy-to-use filing system from scratch.

As the world leaders in filing, the document-organizing experts at Pendaflex are often asked a simple question: "What is the best way to set up a filing system?" Sure, you could just throw a cabinet in the corner, plunk some folders into it and go about your business. However, will you be able to find the documents you want, whenever you want?

Actually, it's quite easy to start a filing system that is certain to work effectively for you every day. And it doesn't matter whether your office is large or small, or even if it's a home office, because the same basic rules apply.

Here are the seven steps I recommend for setting up a new filing system. Follow them, and you'll be amazed how incredibly easy all your filing can be.

1. Begin by placing your file cabinet in an area where you and your co-workers can have clear access to it. Be sure to allow enough room to conveniently open the drawers.
2. The fastest proven method of filing is hanging filing, where folders are suspended on rails and glide along the

rails. If your cabinet does not have built-in rails for hanging folders, put in a "hanging filing frame," which you can buy at any office products retailer.

3. Place your hanging folders on the rails inside the cabinet drawer.

4. Create the headings for your files, using insertable tabs designed specifically for hanging folders. The inserts themselves are available pre-printed with such headings as A–Z or Jan.–Dec., depending on your filing needs. You can also purchase blank inserts for creating your own headings. Or, we also recommend printing your headings using an electronic label printer.

5. Place the tabs onto your hanging folders by inserting the prongs on each tab into the special "teardrop" slots on the top of each folder. Today it's even easier with the new ReadyTab folders from Pendaflex—the tabs are already built in.

6. Prepare interior folders, which are special folders (cut shorter than regular folders) designed to separate and organize papers within hanging folders. As with the headings for your hanging folders, you can also create labels for the interior folders using an electronic labelmaker.

7. Place your labeled interior folders, which come in several colors, into the color-matched hanging folders, and you're done—all ready to file using a complete, super-efficient, hanging filing system!

Dear Sharon:

What is the proper way to set up and maintain a filing system? Are there rules or suggestions for tab placement on hanging file folders, i.e., straight-line tab placement or staggered? Should the hanging file tab be in front or in back? [What is the] proper placement of new records in the file folder, front or back?

Ann, Administrative Assistant

Dear Ann,

Setting up and maintaining a filing system is a broad subject and the answer depends on your recordkeeping needs, such as whether you require a numerical, alphabetical or a combination alpha-numeric system. However, no matter which system you choose, certain rules apply, especially with regard to hanging folders. I recommend that tabs be staggered, simply because they are more visible that way. The tab should always be placed on the front flap of a hanging folder; this eliminates the "push, then pull" routine and allows you to simply pull the tab forward to open the file. As for new records, they should be placed in the front of the folder for fastest access.

The Choice Is Yours

Which filing method is best for you?
Select from three proven approaches.

What kind of filing system is right for your office? Basically, there are three different filing methods (or types of systems) you can choose from. These include filing by "name," by "subject" or by "number." As a general rule, name and subject filing will work fine in almost any office. However, if you have especially large amounts of materials to file, or if the privacy of your files is a concern, numeric filing is probably the best choice for you.

Listed below are short overviews of the three basic filing approaches:

1. **Name filing** means that you set up your files by name alphabetically, like the White Pages of your telephone book. As you might have guessed, name filing is the most popular way to file, probably because it's the easiest. Name filing is best for you if most of your business files are (or will be) arranged by contact name, supplier name, employee name or any other name. It's also the right method to choose for organizing home-office files by such things as the name of your doctor, your accountant or your child's teachers.

2. **Subject filing** is a way of putting similar types of infor- mation into the same group. The Yellow Pages of the

phone book are a good example of subject filing. If your business files depend on what the information is about (such as financial records or marketing reports) rather than who the information is about, subject filing is right for you.

In a home office, you could arrange your files according to subjects covering such topics as automotive repairs, personal taxes and family estate planning.

3. **Numeric filing** means that you set up your files by number, instead of by name or subject. Each number refers to a name or subject that you list in a separate index or register, so you can find the papers you need easily and with pinpoint accuracy. Numeric filing systems are the smart choice if you need a lot of security or privacy in your files, because nobody can tell what's in each numbered file just by opening up a file drawer.

Dear Sharon:

I need tips on setting up an executive filing system. [My boss] is the CFO and we need to make a quick reference system.

Susan M., Administrative Assistant

Dear Susan,

   One of the best ways ever to organize a filing system for quick referencing is to use hanging file folders. I suggest Pendaflex folders; they are stronger and will last longer. Because they hang on rails, the folders always stay neat in the drawer and tabs are always upright and instantly visible. Plus, Pendaflex folders have exclusive InfoPocket™ design—a file-in-a-file for storing related project items such as CDs containing financial data in the same folder with regular papers. To make your boss's filing system even more efficient, add interior folders, designed to subdivide records inside hanging folders. For more filing tips, I invite you to visit *www.pendaflex.com* to view an online version of the official Pendaflex How to File Guide.

The ABCs of Better Filing

Seven important rules to follow when using an alphabetical filing system.

There have been many studies involving the ways in which people file. The most popular method of filing is to arrange folders alphabetically by name, putting the names of people or businesses on folder headings then placing the folders in the drawer according to the alphabet.

Here are seven basic rules for setting up and using an alphabetical name filing system:

1. **Put a person's last name first.** This also applies to businesses named after people. Example, in alphabetical order: "Anderson, Bill" would precede "Cummings, Anne" in the file.

2. **Nothing comes before something.** A last name, when used alone, comes before a last name with a first initial. Example: "Johnson" would precede "Johnson, L." in the file.

3. **Prefixes come before the rest of the name.** Always arrange all prefixes in your file exactly as they are spelled. Example: "Saint John" should be filed as "Saint John," not as "John, Saint."

4. **Spell the name of a business precisely as the business itself spells its own name.** Example: "Smith Manufacturing Company" should be filed as "Smith Manufacturing Company," not as "Smith Company, Manufacturing."

5. **Ignore "The" at the beginning of a name.** Example: "The American Society of Engineering" should be filed alphabetically as "American Society of Engineering, The."

6. **Keep the hyphen** as it appears in hyphenated words. These types of names should be filed as written, example: "Baxter-Brown Associates" should be filed as "Baxter-Brown Associates," not as "Brown Associates, Baxter."

7. **File governmental or political organizations with the major name first.** This is because you'll almost always

look for the information you want under the major name first. Example: "New York Department of Motor Vehicles" should be filed as "Department of Motor Vehicles, New York."

Dear Sharon:

Please advise the correct way to file hyphened last names, for example, Martin-Jones. Some staff file under Martin, some file under Jones. If we knew the correct procedure, we could be consistent in all departments.

Deb, Administrative Assistant

Dear Deb,

You should always file according to the first word that appears in the hyphenated name. In this case, you would file under "M" for Martin.

Location, Location, Location

How to create a geographic file to easily organize contacts by state, city and everywhere in between.

Many companies, possibly yours, have a need to arrange their files according to the geographic location of customers, vendors, business associates and other contacts. For instance, a company's sales regions might be structured into four areas of the country: North, South, East and West, and customer records need to be filed within those respective regions.

If a filing subject's location is the most important thing about the subject, then "geographic filing" is the best system to use. Setting up a geographic file is very simple and it's also extremely easy to use in a busy office.

First, decide what your major filing divisions need to be. If your business is global, you'll need to separate your files by country. Then subdivide by regions, provinces and cities within each country. If you're setting up a geographic file for contacts within the United States, you'll also subdivide your records by state, county, city, town and so on.

Create a separate hanging folder with a location tab for each major division. Depending on the amount of material you need to file and for the most filing efficiency, you may also want to use a separate hanging folder for each subdivision.

Next, use interior folders inside hanging folders to arrange your contacts alphabetically by their respective geographic location.

To add even more filing efficiency and make finding files much faster, use different color hanging folders to designate each major division, and use color-matched interior folders as well. An example of how a geographic file might be arranged for contacts within the United States is as follows: Northeast (major division); New Jersey (subdivision); Trenton (subdivision); Atlas Manufacturing, Benco Associates, Corning Partners (each within its own interior folder).

Another hint: use staggered left-to-right tabbing positions on your hanging folders. This will keep each tab in full view for the quickest fingertip access with much less chance of misfiles.

Now that you've set up your files, maintaining them becomes a high priority.

Account Management

How to set up a customer name file to keep track of key contacts.

Organizing files that contain information relating to your customers may be one of the most important recordkeeping tasks that any business performs. After all, the very existence of just about every business depends upon the ability to meet customer needs.

One of the best ways to ensure that your company serves its customers in a timely and efficient manner is to create what's called a "customer name file" that will allow you to reference filed information about any customer with fingertip ease.

A customer name file is set up much like a personnel file, where individual sections of the filing drawer contain records about a specific alphabetic group of customers and then each drawer section is further broken down into related alpha categories within the main heading.

Customer name files utilize a combination of alphabetic tab headings and numeric tab headings to organize records. Begin by tabbing a separate hanging folder for each letter of the alphabet and depending on the amount of customers you have, break the alpha section down into smaller three-letter groups. For example, if you have a lot of customer names that begin with the letter "A," you might set up an "AMA" tab on a hanging folder, place the folder in your file drawer, and each customer's name that begins with AMA (such as Amalgamated Company and Amarex Consulting Associates) would be placed in that section of the file. In addition to the alphabetical designation, also include a numeric designation on the file tab. Continuing our example, you might assign the number 150 to the "AMA" section of your files and the heading on your file tab would read AMA 150.

Next, label an interior folder for each customer. The tab on the interior folder should contain the name of the customer as well as the corresponding number of the hanging folder. In our example, the interior folder that contains records for the Amalgamated

Company would be labeled as follows: 150 Amalgamated Company. Then place each respective interior folder for each customer alphabetically into its proper hanging folder.

Setting up a customer name file to organize the records of key customer contacts may sound confusing at first, but it's actually quite simple. Best of all, it's a sure way to speed filing time because the combination of alphabetical and numerical tab headings not only gives you a twice-as-fast way to find the records you're looking for, it also helps to prevent misfiles because when used together, alpha and numeric tab designations help ensure that the right records are filed in the right folders.

Put People in Their Place

Tips for creating a personnel file.

Nearly every business has a need for files that organize the records of their employees. Here are some techniques for creating a personnel file that will work seamlessly for almost any business.

Keep in mind that a personnel file is best treated as a name file, whereby employee records are arranged according to last names. Personnel files work best when you use a combination of color-matched hanging folders, tabs and interior folders (interior folders do a great job of subdividing related employee records inside hanging folders).

Start by assigning interior folder and tab colors to each

different department within your company. For example, the marketing department might use red folders and red tabs, engineering might use green and green, and so on. Or, if you prefer, assign according to the different types of employees in your company (full-time, part-time, seasonal, ledger, hourly, etc.).

Then make up a color-matched hanging folder tab for each employee. The tab should show the employee's name, and any other information you deem necessary. Attach each tab to its corresponding-color hanging folder. Next, place each employee's different records in interior folders, and label each interior folder with its proper heading, then place the interior folders in each employee's hanging folder. With all of the new government regulations, it is essential to keep all records confidential.

By using this system, you'll ensure that when any part of any employee's file is out or in transit, the interior folder keeps records confidential, plus, when all information is out, the header tab on the hanging folder still gives you the essential information you need.

Let's now talk about maintaining the folders themselves.

Sort It Out

Presort papers first and turbo-charge filing efficiency.

In many ways, paperwork is like snow—it will accumulate and pile up, if you let it. The key is to file a little at a time, so the task does not become insurmountable. One of the best ways to make filing easier and more efficient is by presorting papers on a regular basis before you put them into the file cabinet.

1. **First things first.** As papers that need to be filed come across your desk, start by prioritizing each document according to its urgency. Papers that are "hot" and must be accessed quickly in the file should be sorted into one group, and papers that can be filed for the long term should be sorted into another.

2. **Assign categories.** How your filing system is set up (alphabetically, numerically, by name, by subject, etc.) will determine another way in which "to-be-filed" papers should be presorted. If for example your system is alphabetical by subject, you should presort your documents into stacks of ready-to-file papers according to what the subject is, such as customer invoices, personnel records, internal memos and so on.

3. **Cherry-pick the bad apples.** At times you will need to file papers that are torn or have crumbled corners. Be sure to presort these into their own group, then repair the damage to the papers before filing. The reason? If you put torn and tattered papers into the file, they will likely ride up in the file drawer and obscure other files, making finding difficult.

4. **Create a separate group for archives.** Many of the papers that need to be filed will never be looked at again, but still need to be kept in the filing system. Presort these papers

into their own group, then put them in a special section of the file cabinet entitled "Archive" files. This will keep archive files out of the way, and make other sections of your file system quicker to locate.

If you follow the simple presorting tips listed above, your entire filing system will work better and easier every day. And although presorting may take a few minutes, the time will be more than made up for, because your files will be efficiently organized for the fastest finding ever!

Annual Rite of Passage

As each year comes to an end, it's time to transfer the files. Here are six ways to make it easy.

At the close of a calendar year, it's time to update your files for the new year: Get rid of what's old and clear space for what will be new in the months to come.

Fact is, to keep your filing system in proper working order throughout the year, it's important that you "purge" the system on an annual basis (or more often if your recordkeeping requirements demand). Dated files can get in the way of current ones, making it difficult to find what you want.

The following are six proven steps for easily transferring this year's files into storage so that you can make room for next year's files.

1. **Make arrangements.** Instead of just randomly pulling old files from the drawer and throwing them into storage, first arrange the files according to date, subject, priority or any other way you want. This will allow you to see exactly what's what before you transfer anything.

2. **Don't be afraid to throw items away.** Chances are, a written recap of the three-legged race at last summer's office picnic is not something you will need for the future. Obviously, you must go through everything carefully, but keep in mind that it's okay to toss records that you're sure are no longer viable—remember, you're trying to make room for new papers that will soon accumulate. As I mentioned before, parting with files is difficult for most people but essential to maintaining order in your files.

3. **Create archive files.** Some papers, even though they're old, still need to be saved for extended periods of time. These might include personnel files or customer billing records. Create separate folders for these files and put them into their own section of your filing system labeled "archives."

4. **Use storage boxes.** A great way to temporarily or permanently store papers that need to be transferred from year to year is to put the papers into corrugated "file storage boxes" specifically designed for that purpose. Your office products retailer has a large selection of these boxes.

5. **Mark contents clearly.** When old files have been transferred into their new storage home, whether it's a corrugated box or an archive drawer, be certain to label the

storage area for fast referencing—you never know when you might need to look something up.

6. **Leave room for expansion.** Chances are, after you think you've finished transferring all your old files, you'll find something else (perhaps another drawer full of records!) that needs to be put into storage. When setting up file storage, be sure to allow extra space for files you might add later on.

Dear Sharon:

I work for the vice chancellor of the Division of Research at a large state university. My question is, I am in the process of rearranging her files and some of them date back to 1995. Can you give me a suggestion on how to archive the old files without using boxes?

Joan, Executive Assistant

Dear Joan,

You say you don't want to use regular boxes to store your old files, so how about an ingenious "box" that's actually a file folder? It's called the Pendaflex Hanging Box File, and it hangs in a file drawer just like regular hanging file folders. It has a squared-off bottom and is extra wide, designed to hold large amounts of papers as well as thick reports, manuals and catalogs. These box files also have closed sides so nothing can fall out of the file and get lost in your file drawer.

To Save or Not to Save

Create a file retention log for tracking what to keep and what to toss.

Among the most common questions people have about filing is how to keep track of what should be saved and what can be thrown away. One of the best, most efficient and easiest ways to keep track of which materials should be retained and which should be tossed is to create a "file retention log."

However, keep in mind that every company and every business is different, and holding on to certain paperwork—or throwing it away—will depend on your company's individual filing requirements.

By creating and utilizing a file retention log in your office, you'll provide yourself and your co-workers with an ongoing working "blueprint" for handling "live" files versus those that are no longer valid.

Here's all you do to create a log yourself. Begin with one or more ring binders, notebooks or several index cards, which will be used to enter and continually update the log information. Once you begin your log, be sure to keep it near the file cabinets for quick referencing, but be certain it's not lost or accidentally thrown away.

Set up the log by entering all the categories of files in your file drawers. Then, and this is the really important part, next to each category, indicate how long each type of record should be kept. In addition, specify how certain records should be handled, that is, should a file be transferred to "archive" after it's gone beyond its retention date, or should it be shredded or simply tossed in the wastebasket?

The Seven Sins of Filing

Avoid these common mistakes, and make all your filing projects easier.

We've all been guilty of them, those easy-to-commit filing errors that can rob your entire office of productivity and, at times, can cause you to work late searching in vain to find a missing document in the file drawer. The following are seven filing miscues that can decrease filing efficiency in a hanging filing system.

1. **Using too few headings.** As a general rule, don't put more than four folders in a row without some sort of subdivision heading.
2. **Using too many folders.** The temptation is to reach for a new folder for every scrap of paper. Whenever possible, do not set up a separate file folder until you have twenty or more papers. To store very small amounts of records, create "miscellaneous" folders.
3. **Folders overstuffed.** We've all done this. Generally, any one folder should not contain more than three-quarter

inches of papers. If you stuff too much into a given folder, papers can ride up and block your file headings, making it nearly impossible to reference something. (For larger filing needs, Pendaflex makes Extra Capacity folders, specially designed for thick filed items.)

4. **Not using interior folders.** These are specifically designed to subdivide related documents inside of hanging folders. Interior folders are cut shorter so they won't obscure hanging folder tabs.

5. **Using worn or torn folders.** Beat-up folders are messy, unsightly and, worse, they can cause misfiles and lost documents. Replace old folders immediately.

6. **Overloading file drawers.** Another temptation most of us have is to jam as much as possible into every nook and cranny of the file drawer. To allow comfortable room to easily get your hands into the drawer so you can access individual files, leave a full four inches of space in each file drawer.

7. **Labeling and tabbing files incorrectly.** One of the best, and most legible ways to label your file folders, especially interior folders, is with DYMO® electronic labeling tools (available wherever office products are sold). Also, when tabbing hanging folders, remember to stagger the tabs across the tops of different folders to provide a clear view of each tab.

Right Now Is the Right Way

Five reasons why filing papers immediately is better than letting them sit idle.

Piles of paperwork are probably among the worst evils in any office. There will always be some active files that you must have accessible. The problem is, today's offices are extremely hectic and most people cannot seem to find the time to file on a regular basis. Therefore, the piles build up, like laundry or dirty dishes, and the more you allow them to build, the harder you make it on yourself and also on your co-workers.

My advice? As difficult as it can be, we suggest filing right away. As I have mentioned before, remember to keep your ACT together: Act, Clear and file or Toss. In other words, as soon as a paper crosses your desk and is ready for the file, put it there. There are several reasons why this strategy is a good one. Here are five of those reasons:

1. **Prevent lost files and misfiles.** The longer a document sits around on a desk, a shelf or anywhere else but in the file, the more chances it has of being misplaced, covered up, hidden or otherwise lost. Furthermore, if you let papers sit idle until you have a mountain of documents to put into the file, misfiles may occur.

2. **Keep confidential information secure.** Many files contain information that is not for everyone's consumption,

such as priority data about budgets as well as personal information about employees and customers. When such papers are allowed to sit instead of being filed immediately, the opportunity for information falling into the wrong hands is increased.

3. **Raise productivity.** If everything that is supposed to be in the file is there when co-workers access the file, less time will be wasted searching for documents in the file drawer. This will help make your department, perhaps your entire company, more efficient and more productive, which in turn will most likely make your job easier.

4. **Avoid confusion.** When papers are placed into the file immediately instead of allowed to sit idle, the chances of confusing documents are decreased substantially. In a file, instead of strewn about the office, each paper is neatly organized in its place, with a file heading that clearly identifies what the file contains.

5. **Create a cleaner desktop.** Rather than letting them pile up on your desk and leaving you with two square inches of workspace, putting papers into the file right away means that you will have more room on your desktop—and that can change your whole outlook every morning when you start your day!

A Matter of Inches

How much is too much to stuff into a file folder?
We answer this and other vital questions.

At some point in your life you've probably "crammed" for a test, and you've likely "stuffed" a turkey for Thanksgiving celebrations. Perhaps you've "overpacked" when going on vacation, and maybe you've "jammed" a basketball. But when it comes to filing, the words cramming, stuffing, overpacking and jamming should not be part of your vocabulary.

Fact is, a file folder that is filled with too much material is extremely hard to reference. Overstuffed papers ride up and hide indexing tabs. Plus, your file drawer becomes so tightly packed that you cannot get your fingers into the drawer in order to find individual papers.

So, now that you know it's counterproductive to fill a file folder with more paper than it's designed to hold, exactly how much is the right amount for each folder? I'm glad you asked. As the world's leading experts in filing, Pendaflex has actually studied the topic extensively, and here are some general rules of thumb that you should follow:

1. **Any one folder should not contain more than three-quarter inches of papers.** When you reach the three-quarter inch limit, either add another folder, or use Hanging Box Bottom Folders with squared-off bottoms for more filing capacity.

2. **Leave a full four inches of space in each file drawer,** giving you room to get your hands into the drawer so you can reach individual folders.

3. **When placing filing cabinets in an office setting, allow a minimum of twenty-four inches** (preferably thirty-six inches to forty-eight inches) to open the drawers. Remember that in order to file efficiently, you must be able to conveniently access each drawer in the cabinet.

4. **When using Extra Capacity Folders, be sure to match the width of the folder (one, two, three or four inches) with the amount of material and thickness of the items you need to file.** Be aware that two inches of paper is perfect for a two-inch box bottom folder, but will flop over in a four-inch box bottom folder.

Cabinet Caveats

Five things to always remember when using a file cabinet.

Most people don't realize it, but a file cabinet is a more intricate piece of office equipment than you might imagine. Indeed, it can save you plenty of time by neatly organizing your filed documents, while also protecting them inside closed drawers. However, a file cabinet must also be used correctly to get the most out of it. Furthermore, it must be used safely to prevent injury to office workers.

The following are five important guidelines to keep in mind concerning each file cabinet in your office:

1. **Never overstuff a cabinet.** The temptation always seems to be to cram as much paperwork as possible into each drawer, but this is counterproductive. Individual papers are much harder to retrieve, mainly because it's very difficult to squeeze your fingers into a jammed-up filing drawer. As a general rule, leave a full four inches of free space in each drawer.

2. **Open only one drawer at a time**, especially the upper drawers. Having several drawers open simultaneously, particularly when a filing cabinet is full, can cause the cabinet to tip over and possibly injure someone.

3. **Label the contents of each file drawer** on the outside front of the drawer; electronic labelmakers and self-stick labels are perfect for this task, providing a visual signal of what each drawer contains. You don't need to include the name of every file in the drawer on your label, just the key categories, which will significantly reduce the time it takes for everyone in your office to find a specific file.

4. **When setting up a cabinet, be sure to leave enough space** in front of the drawers for the drawers to open. This might sound like simple common sense, but it is amazing how often this rule of thinking is ignored.

5. **If your file drawers do not contain built-in rails for hanging filing, put in a frame** specially designed to

convert a standard filing system into a more efficient hanging system. Pendaflex makes several different kinds of frames designed for this purpose.

Tickle Your Fancy

Have daily projects to manage?
Set up a "tickler file" and make your life easier.

Office files and other paperwork will build up, if you let it happen, especially if you're keeping track of documents plus other items such as photos and notes for an ongoing project.

As the project proceeds, the records related to that specific project keep building day by day, and you often find yourself asking "What should I save and what should I throw out?"

An easy way to organize paperwork and related project material on a daily basis is to set up what's called a "tickler file" to temporarily store papers for future use. Here's all you do: Just place a hanging folder in your drawer and also place five interior folders inside the hanging folder.

Label each interior folder with a different day of the week. As the week progresses, drop "papers for review" and other project items such as notes and memos, into the respective interior folders and review all the material at each day's end. On Friday, sort through the entire file to determine what to save and what to transfer to the permanent file. You can also determine at this point what to discard, but be careful about the things you throw away, making sure you won't need those materials later on.

Creating and using tickler files will certainly make your life easier, because a tickler file provides an instant "drop spot" for your current project records, allowing you to quickly organize project material the moment it comes across your desk.

CHAPTER 4

COMPUTER TIPS

Making the Most of Technology

You're stumped, the computer is not cooperating, you're not sure why or where to turn. If you're in my house you turn to your son. People who are young have grown up with the computer but what about the rest of us?

Believe it or not there was a time when we did everything manually; there were no computers and no cell phones. But now the computer is the center of our world at business and it is not uncommon to see people walking around with cell phones or earphones attached to their ears, accessing the Web with their PDAs. In all likelihood, you rely on your computer each and every day, certainly in your office and probably at home as well. Therefore, it's imperative that it not only stays in tip-top working order, but also that you utilize it most effectively. To follow are some computer insights that could be highly valuable to you. These are better solutions than that little voice in your head telling you to toss the computer out the window.

Crash Course

A short lesson in protecting your computer from disastrous crashes.

It's the moment that anyone in the "cyber generation" has come to fear. Your computer hard drive suddenly comes to a halt, completely unresponsive to your mouse clicks and keyboard strokes—and you have tons of data trapped inside. Now what?

This is one of those moments where you need to take a deep breath and keep your ACT together.

First of all, you should never operate your computer for any length of time (more than a day) without backing up your data files. Be sure to regularly copy all your "working" files—such as word processing projects and spreadsheets—onto Zip disks, CDs, DVDs or other external media so that if your computer does crash you will not lose extensive amounts of work.

1. **Why do computer hard drives crash?** We're not talking about a temporary shutdown here, we're talking about a crash that can render your hard drive permanently inoperable. It could be caused by any number of reasons, including old age or faulty manufacturing. However, the

most common causes are electrical "surges" that literally blow out the circuitry and infectious computer "viruses" that invade your hard drive via downloaded Internet files or infected disks.

2. **Surge protectors.** The best way to protect your hard drive from dangerous electrical surges is to use a "surge protector." You simply plug your computer into the protector, then plug the protector into the wall outlet, creating a shield between volatile power surges and your computer hardware.

3. **Antivirus software.** There are many different brands of software on the market specifically created to do battle with computer viruses and automatically eliminate a wide range of viruses from your system. Be sure to purchase a brand that allows you to periodically go onto the company's Web site and download the latest updates designed to kill new viruses.

4. **Anti-crash and recovery software.** In addition to antivirus software, there are also several software utilities available that allow you to prevent individual programs from crashing and recover lost data in the event a program does crash. Anti-crash and recovery software is well worth the money, as it provides added peace of mind "just in case."

Digital Do's (and Do Nots)

**Three smart ways to protect computer data
and two things to avoid.**

We depend on our computers for virtually every aspect of our business lives. And sometimes we take them for granted. We simply think that every time we boot up the computer in the morning, it will be ready to work for us, and we can just continue with our word processing or spread sheet documents right where we left off the day before.

Unfortunately, that's not always the case. There are those days when we can't get ourselves motivated; similarly, computers, as many people have witnessed firsthand, do occasionally stop working—leaving valuable data trapped inside.

Here are three easy steps you can take to protect your computer data:

1. **Back up your files regularly.** Copy your working files each day, or at minimum once a week, from your hard drive onto external media such as Zip disks or CDs.

2. **Turn off your computer when you leave the office for the night.** This is especially important if you have a cable hookup for your online connection. Cable modems are always "on" and thus your computer is a sitting duck for online "hackers."

3. **Use a battery backup or UPS (uninterrupted power**

supply). Your computer plugs into one of these, and, in the event of a power failure, the UPS allows you time to safely save your data and shut down the computer.

Here are two things you should avoid in order to protect your computer data:

1. **Never run an unknown "executable" program.** Executable files, which end with the extension ".exe," can wreak havoc with your computer system if you don't know the origin of the file. Unknown executable files may contain viruses, and many people download them unwittingly, only to find their entire hard drive destroyed when the file is deployed.

2. **Stay away from Internet service providers you're not sure about.** There are many ISPs to choose from today, and many are great but some are not. Fact is, some ISPs do not offer "firewall" protection that helps prevent computer hackers from accessing your hard drive.

Intrusive Behavior

Internet invaders are on the rise; protect your computer data by using firewalls.

Perhaps you have a cable-based online hookup or some other kind of "broadband" Internet connection in your home or your home office. As opposed to a dial-up connection, your computer is always online, and it could possibly be wide open to someone who might want to invade your hard drive and delete some of your files. Or worse, place a "virus" into your computer that could render it inoperable.

A great way to protect your data is to use what is called a firewall, which is software designed to automatically protect your computer system from unwanted intrusion via the Internet. (It's likely that in your office at work, your company has firewall protection already installed in all of the company's computers.)

In simplest terms, firewall software works by preventing unwanted or unsolicited "scans" of your computer's data by other people who are also connected to the Internet. Besides what can potentially come into your computer, outbound information is also monitored by firewall software, which can assist in helping to identify if "spyware" software is invading the data you send.

It all may sound a little high tech and even confusing, but all you really need to remember is that installing firewall software on your computer is probably a very smart idea. There are many firewall products available and your local computer products retailer can explain them in detail.

Creepy Crawlers

How to prevent computer "worm" viruses from destroying your hard drive.

Perhaps this has happened to you or someone in your office: You attempt to boot up your computer in the morning and it starts to respond . . . then, nothing. Or, your computer inexplicably "crashes" in the middle of a task and will not come back to life, no matter what you do. Chances are, you and your computer are the victim of a computer virus.

Recent forms of cyber viruses are especially nasty, and they can enter your hard drive in a number of ways, such as by downloading files from the Internet.

More and more, offices in companies throughout the world are having their hard drives infested by a creative little creature that attaches himself to Internet e-mail and wreaks havoc with any hard drive he enters. He's called a "worm" and he's truly a parasite that eats computer files for breakfast, lunch and dinner.

By way of explanation, a "worm" is actually a series of computer codes programmed to erase or scramble certain files on your hard drive and render them unusable, so your computer can no longer work properly. Typically, a worm will enter your computer disguised as a harmless e-mail greeting, but once he's inside, he will slither around until he's chewed up vital booting and operating files on your hard drive.

Here are some preventive measures for dealing with "worm" viruses:

✓ **Know your source.** If you receive an e-mail that appears suspicious, it indeed may be. Yes, it's difficult to screen every e-mail you receive, but at least be aware of e-mail messages that seem to spell trouble.

✓ **Arm yourself with antivirus software.** As we said in a previous article in this guide, there are several outstanding antivirus software programs available. These products are specifically designed to extinguish known viruses. Most offer free updates from the company's Web site so that you can download updated protective shields that will do battle with new viruses as they appear.

✓ **Avoid the dreaded ".exe" factor.** As also mentioned previously, many computer viruses are created using the extension .exe, which makes them appear to be actual applications. If you receive an e-mail that contains an attached file ending in .exe, do not open that file unless you are absolutely sure the file is safe.

Words to the Wise

Smart word processing tips to make your life easier.

If your job calls for extensive time spent at a computer keyboard working with a word processing program, you're probably constantly looking for intelligent ways to make the task go more smoothly and with less effort.

Here are some straightforward, and very useful, tips for getting the most out of your word processing projects:

✓ **Take advantage of automatic features.** Virtually all of today's leading word processors come with special time-saving shortcuts that allow you to perform certain functions automatically. These include auto formatting of such things as paragraphs, columns, lists and bulleted copy. By utilizing these features you'll instantly make yourself more productive at the keyboard.

✓ **Get a good copyholder.** Besides keeping your hands free for faster typing, you'll keep the copy at a comfortable height—eye level is best. There are several kinds of copy-holders to choose from, including desktop models and models that clip onto your computer monitor.

✓ **Get a keyboard template for quick reference.** Templates are available for all major word processing software programs, and the template itself fits over your keyboard and tells you instantly which keys to use for certain word processing functions. That way, you won't waste time looking things up in the manual.

Process More Words, More Easily

Automate word processing tasks using macros and simplify your life.

When it comes to computer software, one of the best ways to make your life easier is to take full advantage of the software's automated features. A perfect example is the "macro" feature built into just about every word processing program on the market. You may be saying to yourself, *I've heard the term macro, but I'm not exactly sure what it means, let alone what it does.*

Simply put, a macro is a shortcut, a way of automating repetitive word processing procedures and commands so you can perform them with a single keystroke or click of a mouse—making your software easier and faster to use!

For example, let's say you're typing up a list of customer names and addresses and you want the name of each customer to appear bold. Simply assign a "style" macro to the word processing file and all names will become bold with a single keystroke, rather than having to highlight each name individually and then apply bold to it.

Another example would be creating a macro that will automatically insert tables (such as listings of sales figures or financial numbers) into your word processing document. You custom-create the macro and tell it to assign a specific number of rows, columns and borders to each table and then every time you want to put a table into your document, the macro will do the formatting of the table for you.

Macros and the exact ways they work can differ with each software package. However, how to use macros is fully explained in the software documentation. We admit, you might find macros somewhat confusing at first, but once you see how much time they can save you by automating word processing tasks that you would otherwise manually repeat over and over, you'll start using macros more and more!

Key Attributes

Sometimes, using keyboard shortcuts can be quicker than using a mouse.

Sure, a computer mouse is easy to use. However, when you're busy at your keyboard—typing away in a word processing program and trying to get your boss's report done before 5 P.M.—many times it can be even easier and faster to finish the project if you don't have to remove your hands from the keyboard in order to operate the mouse.

To follow are a few "keyboard shortcuts" that will work with most word processing software, including Microsoft Word. All you do is simultaneously press the "Ctrl" key plus another key to perform each function. Try them out for yourself; you might just save a whole lot of time.

- ✓ Ctrl + A —automatically highlights all text in the document.
- ✓ Ctrl + B—applies bold to highlighted text.

✓ Ctrl + C—allows highlighted text to be "copied" so that it can be "pasted" somewhere else in the document (to paste, press Ctrl + V).

✓ Ctrl + I— applies italic to highlighted text.

✓ Ctrl + N—allows you to create a new document.

✓ Ctrl + O—starts the "open" file dialog box, allowing you to access other files on your hard drive.

✓ Ctrl + S—saves the work in the document you are currently working with.

✓ Ctrl + Home—takes you to the beginning of the document.

✓ Ctrl + End—takes you to the end of the document.

In the Key of F

See those "F" keys on the top of your computer keyboard? They can save you time; here's how.

If, for example, you're working on a personal computer using a Windows-based word processing program, you will notice keys at the top of your keyboard that begin with the letter "F."

These are the "function" keys or "F keys." Depending on your software, you could bypass the mouse completely when running "spell-check" and just press F7. Or, you could view an instant thesaurus by pressing F12. And, you could print your document simply by pressing F4.

With a mouse, all of these functions would probably take a minimum of two or three clicks . . . that is, once you remove your hands from the keyboard (where you're already typing), find the mouse button and position the pointer arrow over the on-screen function you want to access.

In addition to the use of F keys alone, certain keyboard short-cuts may also give you even more possibilities to perform quick computer functions by asking you to combine the pressing of an F key with another key, such as the "Ctrl" or "Alt" key. For instance, by pressing "Ctrl + F6" you might be able to bring up a dialog box that lets you change fonts instantly in your document.

Check your software documentation for specific ways that you can utilize the F keys on your computer keyboard to make your job easier.

Dear Sharon:

It's been so long since I've taken Clerk Typing and Stenography, and I rarely do filing of personal names. Nevertheless, my job requires that I do enter information in the computer, last name first, etc. I've run across a situation in which two last names are used, and I'm not quite sure how to do the filing. For example: Mary Jane Smith-Jones. I thought it would be Jones Smith Mary Jane, but it seems I recall from high school it should be Jones Mary Jane Smith. Can you refresh my memory? I sure would appreciate help on this. Thanks so much!

Andi, Document Control Clerk

Dear Andi,

Great question, and it's one that many people often struggle with. You're right about the fact that when filing, you always put a person's last name first. However, the hyphen in hyphenated names should be ignored. So, in the case of your example, Mary Jane Smith-Jones should be filed as "Smith-Jones, Mary Jane." A great suggestion—when in doubt always refer to the phone book.

Now Boarding: You and Your Laptop

Five suggestions for checking your notebook computer through heightened airport security.

Obviously, there is more focus on security at airports than ever before. Carry-on items are subject to incredible scrutiny, and, for the millions of business travelers who have become accustomed to toting along their laptop computers when they fly, the increase in security has prompted significant changes in pre-boarding procedures.

The following are five simple suggestions for moving your portable computer equipment through airport security with fewer hassles and less worry:

1. **Do not be concerned about putting your notebook computer through the airport's X-ray machine.** Even though some X-ray machines may be more sensitive than they were in the past, any computer expert you ask will tell you that running your computer through an X-ray checkpoint will not damage the computer.

2. **Do not turn your laptop computer on before going through airport security, unless you are specifically asked to do so.** There's no reason to take a chance that your data could be disrupted or your computer's operating features could be jeopardized simply because the computer is turned on as it's being checked.

3. **Be prepared to remove your laptop from its case.** Today's airport security often involves agents physically looking inside carry-on luggage. Mainly because you'll be more careful with your expensive piece of equipment than an agent is likely to be, it's better that you remove the computer yourself, so remember to keep at least one hand free to handle your computer.

4. **Don't lose sight of your laptop as it moves through security.** Newly expanded security procedures have resulted in a certain amount of confusion at airport gates, and that has created opportunities for thieves to steal valuable computer gear.

5. **Identify your laptop and its case clearly, perhaps by putting a piece of brightly colored tape on each piece of your equipment.** Once again, in the confusion that has

been created by new and more extensive security procedures, some business travelers find themselves picking up
the wrong notebook computer after passing through a
security checkpoint.

You've Got Mail, Now What?

Five smart tips for managing the flood of e-mail we all have to deal with these days.

For most computer users, the computer's in box is constantly filled
with tons of e-mails. And the challenge of keeping track of it all is not
limited to the business office. In fact, many people receive much more
e-mail on their home computers than they do in the office. Either
way, you need a plan to prevent dealing with the buildup of e-mails
from becoming a full-time job. Here are five easy suggestions:

1. **Create a special computer folder to temporarily store the
   e-mail files you receive.** Many Internet services automatically send your e-mails directly to a "download" folder or
   some other e-mail in-box folder on your hard drive. The
   trick is not to let the download folder get overloaded with
   too many e-mailed files. By creating a dedicated digital
   folder just for e-mails you want to save, you'll always know
   right where to access those important e-mails.

2. **Delete e-mails you know you will not need.** Avoid letting
   electronically-mailed files remain for too long in your

computer. You'd be surprised how quickly your hard drive can get crowded with these files, and you also may not realize that the speed of your computer could actually be slowed down by too many e-mails stored in your computer system. If you're not sure whether you need to save an e-mail message or an attached file, copy it onto a floppy or burn a CD before deleting from your hard drive. You can then always go back and review the e-mail later.

3. **Before downloading "just any" e-mail, be sure you really want to download it and that it is safe to do so.** Often in the office, and certainly many times at home, you are likely to get bombarded with all kinds of e-mails from sources you may not recognize. Not only do many of these electronic messages usually contain attachments that can clutter your hard drive, sometimes they may even include dangerous viruses that can destroy your computer system. A simple rule of thumb: if you don't recognize the sender of the e-mail as some sort of business contact or other person you might know, it's probably best to simply delete the message and not download it at all.

4. **Keep business and personal e-mails separate.** In addition to receiving e-mail messages from co-workers, customers and other business contacts, many people also get e-mails sent to them at work from friends and relatives. If you do save personal e-mail files, be sure to place them in a different digital folder than your business e-mails to avoid confusion.

5. **Respond immediately.** Many e-mails require that you reply to them in some way. Do not delay in doing so, simply because the amount of e-mail messages builds throughout the day, and many responses can be forgotten or overlooked.

Dear Sharon:

I have always printed my boss's e-mail and sorted incoming mail. I have a "Monday" folder, "Tuesday" folder, etc. There are days when my boss does not have the time to go through all of this paperwork and I feel like I am constantly chasing him down for a response to something that was in the "Monday" folder. Does anyone have any suggestions? I thought of labeling the folders as follows: Needs Signature, Needs Attention, Corporate Reports and perhaps a folder labeled General Info for all the magazines, promotions/re-org announcements, e-mail, FYIs, etc. Has anyone tried this? Would you have another suggestion that may be best suited for us?

Terri, Administrative Assistant

Dear Terri,

It's a good thing there are only five work days in a week. Your idea about labeling the folders with different "take-action" headings is a good one. One of the best ways to create the labels themselves is by using an electronic labeling tool that prints high quality labels in several colors. An example of such a product is a DYMO® brand electronic labeler, which you could use to print bright, attention-getting labels that communicate things like "Immediate Response Needed." Another possibility is the Pendaflex Project Sorter, it has ten color-coded sections with blank tabs that you can customize. Another solution would be to create folders on your computer instead of printing all of the e-mails and forward them with the appropriate headings. Your boss may respond to an e-mail faster rather than reading through so much paperwork.

E-Mail E-tiquette

Reply or forward? Four ways to practice good manners with electronic mail.

As you well know, working in today's high-tech office means tons and tons of e-mails exchanged between co-workers, departments, branches, customers and other business associates.

And while most people extend the same kind of etiquette to creating and sending electronic mail as they would to regular postal delivered "snail mail," e-mail tends to be less formal and because it is much more immediate, certain levels of courtesy are sometimes overlooked.

Here are four easy approaches to e-mail etiquette:

1. **Ask before you forward.** Resist the temptation to automatically forward someone else's e-mail that may have been originally intended only for you. Sure, it's easy to just click your mouse and send the e-mail on to co-workers, but first, be sure that the sender is okay with that.

2. **Minimize the reply chain.** Too often in business, e-mails are created then the same e-mail is replied to and forwarded over and over again with new messages added each time. Problem is, in order to read the most recent message, you have to weed through all the preceding messages. Whenever possible, create a new e-mail that eliminates this ever-growing chain of previous messages.

3. **Be businesslike in your writing.** It can be easy with e-mail to slip into the same informal writing style you might use online with instant messaging. Remember that your business e-mails should be every bit as businesslike as a paper office memo or letter you might create. So avoid catchy "cyber abbreviations," "smiley faces" made with punctuation marks and other approaches that could be perceived as less than professional.

4. **Do not make a habit of trivializing.** Everyone enjoys the occasional "fun" e-mail sent by a co-worker, the one that tests your trivia knowledge or tells a joke. However, some office workers abuse the power of e-mail and send non-stop barrages of these types of electronic correspondences to their work associates—clogging up a person's day with a continual stream of non-business transmissions. Remember that although there's always room for some fun in the office, people are busy and opening an e-mail requires time from your recipient.

Dear Sharon,

I have a ton of paper to file and I'm not sure what the best way would be to file it. These are pages that I have copied from the Internet and from my online friends and/or family members. I don't know if they should be filed by the sender's name, Web address, or by topic. Some of the copies consist of more than one subject. Some of the copies are jokes, stories, recipes, important information, personal information, etc. I would like to be able to retrieve them from time to time but I want them to be easy to find. Can you help me solve this problem before I get started? I would really appreciate this very much.

Ghayle, Retired Senior Stenographer

Dear Ghayle,

I seem to get more and more requests for advice about filing printed information obtained from the Internet. It's hard to believe that many people once predicted computers would create a digital "paperless office." Instead, the exact opposite has happened and due in large part to the seemingly endless array of Web pages out there, we have more paper than ever to organize. Here is my suggestion: Set up an alphabetical filing system using different folders for each of the different "topics" you have. For example, in alphabetical order, the tab on your first folder would be "Jokes," the second folder would be tabbed "Important Information," the third would be tabbed "Personal Information" and so on. Organizing files alphabetically, in both homes and in offices, is the most popular method because it's the easiest to set up and maintain; as you gather new papers just add them to the applicable alphabetic folder. Also, by breaking each of your categories into its own alphabetized folder, you "divide and conquer" your overall filing system, making individual categories and papers faster to find.

Of Mice and Moan

**Using the wrong computer mouse can
be painful. Here's how to pick the right one.**

Office professionals typically spend hour after hour, every single day, at a computer, constantly typing and also clicking away at a mouse. Problem is, most of us simply accept and use the mouse that comes with the computer. In fact, we don't even give it a second thought.

However, did you know that a computer mouse that is uncomfortable for your hand could eventually be a contributing factor in repetitive stress syndrome or some other form of severe hand pain? It's true. Studies among office workers have shown that repetitive-stress injuries are most likely to occur from small, repeated movements—much like the movements you would perform when working with a mouse. Adding to the situation is the fact that many of today's graphic-rich computer programs, with numerous "point-and-click" icons, require continual mouse commands.

Here are some simple suggestions to consider in choosing a computer mouse:

✓ **Go bigger.** You might think that the smaller the mouse, the easier it is to control. But in fact, the opposite is true for most people. A larger mouse requires less clutching, can be more ergonomic overall, and also can cover more ground on your mouse pad with less movement.

✓ **Go optical.** The typical mouse utilizes a roller ball to track and operate. An alternative, and probably a better one, is a mouse that uses a light sensor instead of a ball to track its position. Most times, these optical mice do not even require a mouse pad, and, they tend to track more consistently. Over time, this can eliminate thousands and perhaps hundreds of thousands of extra movements you might have to make with a traditional ball-tracking mouse.

✓ **Go longer.** Many times, people will find that the cord that connects a mouse to the computer is too short, requiring constant readjusting or tugging to pull the mouse into the most comfortable position for use. Consider a mouse extension cord, available at any computer store for about $10. Another consideration, if you want to spend a few more bucks, would be a cordless mouse that uses a radio transmitter to communicate with your computer.

All Hands on Tech

Five easy tips for getting the most
out of the technology in your office.

There was a time when many people, especially those of us who have worked in an office for a long time, viewed technology as just a little intimidating. Now, all of us (or at least most of us) have embraced electronic wizardry as a way to help us work more productively in offices both large and small.

However, are you utilizing the power of technology to its fullest? Or, are you sometimes frustrated when something electronic seems to have a mind of its own and causes you undue stress?

The following are some tips for enhancing, and expanding, the way you use office technology:

1. **Do you have a scanner hooked up to your computer?** If so, you have a handy desktop copy machine. Many people don't realize that in addition to scanning photos, these versatile tools can also produce instant photocopies through your printer.

2. **When using e-mail, "reply" sparingly.** We've all received those seemingly endless e-mail messages that have been replied to and forwarded many times before they get to us, meaning that you have to plow through all the previous messages to read the latest one. Whenever possible, try not to perpetuate the "reply and forward" confusion, and you will make your e-mail communications more effective.

3. **Does your computer freeze up now and then?** PCs have a built-in way to "restart" them, in most cases allowing you to at least get your computer going again. All you do is simultaneously press the Alt, Ctrl and Delete keys.

Remember though, that restarting your computer means that whatever you have not saved prior to the restart will probably be lost.

4. **When leaving a message on an electronic office voice-mail system, state the purpose of your message.** Instead of just saying that you called, explain briefly what the call is about. Studies have shown that in most cases, when people know the reason why a message is left, they will call back faster.

5. **Want a sure way to make certain your faxes are received completely?** On your fax cover sheet, always indicate how many pages are contained in the fax (including the cover sheet itself). That way, you and your recipient will know that they have gotten the entire fax.

CHAPTER 5

PRODUCTIVITY ENHANCERS

Work Smarter Not Harder

Do you ever wonder why it is that, despite working so hard, you seem to be continually behind in the amount of work you actually finish? It can leave you scratching your head. It's all about productivity, which simply means going about your work in the most efficient way. The following are some straightforward suggestions for handling deadlines and projects that you can put into practice easily, just by following the ACT philosophy.

Efficiency Expertise

Ways to put more productivity into every hour.

You look at the clock. It's 4:00 in the afternoon and you're going home in one hour. Problem is, you have two hours' worth of work left. Where did the day go? Why is there never enough time to do your job?

Without question, the office world is moving faster than ever before. Circumstances such as lightning-quick Internet connections, high-speed fax machines and growing global business competition have forced everyone to step up the pace—and that's putting great pressure on all of us to keep up.

To avoid going nuts and falling behind with your work, you need to find ways to become more productive. In other words, to do more in less time.

Here are some suggestions for increasing your work productivity:

1. **Put everything in its place.** A messy workspace, especially a cluttered desk, can cost you minutes every day and hours every week, simply because you'll waste time looking for things.

2. **Apply a method to the madness.** It's important to establish a system for everyday tasks such as filing or distributing office memos. Once you have a good working system in place, you won't waste time looking for better ways to accomplish those tasks.

3. **Focus your thoughts.** When you begin something, work toward finishing it—rather than skipping all over the place trying to juggle your attention among many tasks. Staying focused on the job at hand makes you much more productive simply because you'll have less chance of making time-consuming mistakes.

4. **Don't sweat the small stuff.** Try to avoid laboring over every tiny detail, such as whether a letter should be typed with a half-inch indent or three-quarters. Perfectionism can be a source of procrastination.

5. **Take a breather.** It is imperative that you refresh yourself periodically, and not just during scheduled breaks or at lunch. You'll be amazed how a few moments of looking out the window can give you new energy and make you more productive and efficient overall.

Dear Sharon:

This is actually a suggestion for admins to help their bosses. My boss tends to put EVERYTHING in one or two piles on his desk, and then can't find ANYTHING! What I have started doing to help him out is take the piles and create folders for each item or group of items in the pile. Then he ends up with a stack of file folders on his desk instead of papers, and it makes it much easier for him to find what he is looking for. It seems to make his working life easier and more organized. Hope this suggestion helps someone!

Deanna, Executive Administrator

Dear Deanna,

Ah, I see my message is getting through loud and clear: Do not let piles of paperwork build up because eventually the piles become insurmountable and important documents get lost. Thanks so much for reinforcing the advice I've offered several times in this column and utilizing it in your own office to turn disorganized mountains of paper into more organized file folders. However, there are times when active files are best kept on the desk. I would like to make one suggestion; why not take your filing efficiency a step further and put the folders themselves into a desktop organizer such as the Pendalflex® Project Sorter, or use Pendaflex PileSmart™ write-on clips to keep track of desktop files. The innovative folders and clips make it easy to find any active files.

First Things First

The importance of prioritizing

No matter how many hands you think you have, or how many projects you think you can juggle, no one can do everything all at once.

That's why it's so important to prioritize—and one of the best ways to do it is by making lists, in priority order, of the projects you're working on. Multitasking does not mean working on two projects at the exact same time. Of course, due dates are a critical factor in determining which projects should be addressed first, but you also need to consider other things, such as:

1. **Approximately how much time will I need to finish a particular project?** Obviously, the ones that will take longer need to be started earlier.

2. **How involved is the approval process?** If many people need to review the project you're creating, you need to allow time for everyone to put their two cents in.

3. **How vital is the project itself?** Naturally, a new business proposal you're developing for your boss would take priority over the office pool you're setting up for next year's Super Bowl.

4. **How visible is the project?** Let's face it, if the feasibility study you're helping your boss put together will eventually land on the desk of the CEO, the project is highly visible.

If you keep each of the above things in mind, prioritizing will be much easier—which in turn will make it easier to stay on schedule day after day and week after week.

There's No Time Like the Present

Avoiding procrastination—six ways to "do it now!"

We're all guilty of putting things off. It's just human nature. However, in today's busy office environment, procrastination can cause costly backups in workflow, eventually snowballing into a situation that will undoubtedly anger your boss.

Here are six easy-to-follow tips for avoiding the inevitable urge to wait until tomorrow for something you can get done today (let's leave tomorrow to Scarlett O'Hara):

1. **Consider your time restraints.** No one can do everything all at once, so it's important to address the most time-sensitive tasks first. If the sales report is due Tuesday and the follow-up letter to the customer is due Wednesday, obviously you need to work on the report first.

2. **Make a list.** Each morning when you come into the office, or even the night before, write down all the projects you need to complete by day's end. This will provide a tangible blueprint for you to follow throughout the day in order to get things done. As each task is completed, cross it off the list. Your daily diary is one of your most important tools.

3. **Establish obtainable goals.** Don't set yourself up for failure. Of course, your boss may occasionally load you down with more work than you can complete in a given time frame, but usually, we contribute most to procrastination by thinking we can accomplish more than we realistically can. It's also important to let your boss know that the time frame is not realistic and offer a solution.

4. **Don't create a catastrophic atmosphere for yourself.** Sometimes, we can subconsciously slow our work pace

down, even frighten ourselves, by anticipating failure. Think positive thoughts when working on a project—you can complete it on time, and you will. But if you don't, it's not the end of the world.

5. **Leave constant reminders.** Notes placed strategically on bulletin boards, on your computer monitor and other visible places will continually remind you of the tasks that need to be completed, helping you avoid putting things off.

6. **Reward yourself for a job well done.** When you complete a task, congratulate yourself. If possible, treat yourself to a short break. You earned it!

Try each of the above techniques for avoiding procrastination. In fact, try them today!

 Perfect Timing

Proven tips for meeting deadlines

Deadlines appear to have gotten shorter. A few years ago, your boss may have needed you to complete a big project in a month; now, he or she is demanding that you finish the project in a week. Or less.

How do you keep up? How do you meet nearly impossible deadlines? Here are a few common-sense tips:

1. **Establish a plan of attack.** Proceeding headlong without preparation is a sure recipe for disaster. Before beginning a project, write down all the things you need to accomplish. This will provide a tangible overview you can follow in completing the assignment on time.

2. **Put all the elements in place.** After you've gathered your thoughts, gather all the things you will need to finish the project. For instance, if you will need binders to house the engineering report you're preparing for your boss, get the binders ahead of time—and the paper that will go in the binders—and the labels for the outside of the binders.

3. **Divide and conquer.** Separate the many aspects of a project into smaller parts and you'll make the job less intimidating and easier to finish on time. For instance, you might be asked to reorganize your entire department's filing system. Divide the files into sections, perhaps by customer, and finish each section before moving on to another part of the file.

4. **Proceed with caution.** Yes, the deadline is tight, but rushing carelessly and making mistakes will only cost you more time doing things over. Staying focused is one of the best ways to stay on schedule when you're up against a tight deadline.

Back to Business

At the end of every year, we celebrate the holiday, but returning to your regular work routine can be hard. Here's some advice.

The holiday season always has plenty of hustle and bustle, including attending parties and eating enough delectable foods to last you all the way to next year. Once the festive holiday season has passed, however, there can be a little bit of a letdown. And it can be difficult to get back into the normal grind of work after your attention has been diverted by a constant stream of holiday cards, luncheons with co-workers and shopping for presents.

Here are three simple tips for resuming your daily work routine without going out of your mind:

1. **Remove the reminders.** This doesn't mean to sound like it came from Scrooge himself, but it's a good idea to take down all holiday decorations as soon as the holiday season is over. Sure, they look great and they're colorful, but they can also be distracting, preventing you from settling in to the work demands of a new year.

2. **Look forward.** The end of a year is a great time to update the files by setting up new folders for the new year while also archiving some of your current year's records. You might also create files for future years, say two or three years down the road, depending on your business. This is

a great time to set up the file for next year's taxes.

3. **Pace yourself.** More likely than not, some work backed up during the past holiday season. Be careful not to overextend yourself by doing too much to catch up. Yes, you'll have to work a little harder to offset holiday downtime, but don't try to be a super-person, taking the chance of burning yourself out, which will make it that much harder to return to your pre-holiday routine.

Office Interruptus

How to prevent distractions from interrupting your workday.

See if this scenario sounds familiar: You're rushing to get a project done before you go home, when suddenly the phone rings, interrupting your workflow. Or, you have a deadline to put a report together and you're scrambling to finish it, when a co-worker decides to stop by your desk to tell you a story about her kids, distracting your concentration.

These are common office interruptions and they can rob you of productivity—if you let them. Here are some simple, yet effective, ways to help keep your mind on your work:

Let the machine get it. Of course, your job may involve answering the phone and taking messages; however, if you're working on a special project with a deadline, it's probably best to let your electronic voice mail handle the call so you don't have to stop what you're doing midstream to answer the phone.

Do not disturb. Perhaps more office efficiency is lost due to "office chatting" than to anything else. And while we're not saying you should avoid co-workers and be a non-social person, sometimes you simply need to be alone in order to get your work done. If someone (other than your boss) tries to interrupt you while you're rushing to complete a project, don't be afraid to politely tell them that you're extremely busy at the moment and you don't have time to talk right now.

Avoid wandering thoughts. Daydreaming can be quite tempting, but unfortunately it's another surefire way to reduce the productivity in your workday. Indeed, your mind may continually want to wander away from the task at hand, but if you let it, your concentration can easily be broken and you'll likely make mistakes, causing even more downtime by having to do things over.

Clear the clutter. If you have to clear a space on your desk every time you want to do something, or if you have to search for lost items in the middle of a project, your productivity will suffer. Keep your work area clutter free and you'll be surprised how much more you can accomplish in less time.

Dear Sharon:

Thank you for making my life easier! I work with all male nuclear physicists. I used to mysteriously "lose" file folders, notes, pens, staplers, tape, etc., but since I've changed everything to the color pink (love those pink file folders), they won't touch anything on my desk! It seems they don't want to be caught dead with anything pink! Haven't lost any pink things since.

Jeannette, Administrative Assistant

Dear Jeannette,

Thanks for the kind words. And, thanks for helping to promote the importance of using colored filing products such as pink folders (with all due respect to our many male I Hate Filing Club members)!

Cubic Feat

Work in a cubicle? Here's how to accomplish more by minimizing disruptions.

Office cubicles are a fact of life in just about every company, and millions of people work in them. While we've all come to accept the office cubicle as a "fixture" of the modern business environment, there can be drawbacks to working in one.

For example, they can lack privacy simply because they are basically open—usually with no doors and with walls that only reach partially to the ceiling. At times, the inherent design of a cubicle can be a detriment to working productively, negatively affecting the ability of office workers to obtain daily goals such as meeting deadlines.

The following are some straightforward tips that could help your office accomplish a higher level of productivity despite the distractions that come with working in a cubicle:

1. **Keep the noise level down.** As you might guess, one of the biggest detriments to working in a cubicle is the fact that because they're not soundproof it's easy to be distracted by too much noise. Be courteous to your fellow workers and encourage them to do the same by avoiding the use of radios or CD players. Also, be aware of the volume of your voice when on the telephone and try to avoid "shouting over the walls" to fellow workers.

2. **Create visual barriers.** Many office cubicles have particularly low walls that provide very little privacy. Try stacking books on shelves near the top of the wall to effectively increase the height of the wall. Also try to position your chair so that you can see someone entering your space. Try not to have your back to the entrance of your space.

3. **Remember that neatness counts, especially in a cubicle.**

Most cubicles are limited in the amount of space in which they allow you to work. As I often mention try not to accumulate too much extraneous "stuff" that can cause your workspace to become messy and more crowded than it already is. For example, if you receive a box from the mail room, remove what you need and discard the box. Also, do not allow paperwork to build up. File as soon as you possibly can.

Time Is of the Essence

Are you more productive in the A.M. or P.M.? Let's explore the best times to tackle certain projects.

Of course, if your office is like most, you're constantly busy working on something. And as a result of today's frenzied office schedules, you cannot always choose the time of the day that you will approach all your projects.

However, with the right planning, you can control whether you work on certain projects in the morning or in the afternoon, at the beginning of the week or at the end. You may be surprised to learn that it actually makes a difference. In fact, I have checked with several efficiency experts and they report that you can substantially increase your productivity by scheduling various tasks at times that are best suited for each task.

Here are some suggestions:

1. **Beginning a new project.** It seems logical that the best time to start a project is at the beginning of the week. Yet, this is not the case. Statistics show that most people handle new assignments best on Wednesday. Maybe it's the psychological aspects of knowing that it's "hump day" and you're halfway to the weekend. Mondays and Fridays are the worst days to start new projects.

2. **Following up on a "working" project.** This is best on a Thursday, in the morning. That way, you or the people you're following up with will have time to take any necessary steps before the week is over.

3. **Filing.** Although filing is a necessary evil for most people, it's not a task that requires a lot of energy, or for that matter, thinking. Therefore, the experts suggest that office filing is done in the afternoon, when energy levels and thought power are usually somewhat lower than they would be in the morning.

4. **Writing a letter.** This is definitely an activity that you should schedule for the morning, preferably at the beginning of the week. Studies prove that most people are more creative during the morning hours. In addition, they are rested from the weekend at the start of a given week—allowing for better processing of thoughts in order to craft a more powerful letter.

5. **Asking for a raise.** There's a reason why many of the most important business deals are accomplished in a restaurant—people are more friendly and more receptive to

suggestions when they have a full stomach. With that in mind, it's best to approach your boss about a salary increase right after lunch.

The Power of Positive Persuasion

How to prevent negative thinking from thwarting office productivity.

Think about it and you'll likely agree—in every office there seems to be at least a few people who are constantly complaining about something. Nothing ever seems to make them happy and at times, the negative aura that they bring to an office can be infectious, spreading to co-workers.

Maybe these people are complaining about the amount of work they have to do, or perhaps they're not happy with the salary they're making, or maybe they don't like the long hours. Whatever the complaint, the effect is usually unproductive, often causing an office work team to go about their business with less energy and commitment than they would have in a positive working environment.

The following are some simple tips for addressing the problem of negative thinking in your office:

1. **Recognize the signs.** The first thing you need to do is realize that negativity is indeed present. Among the surest signs are people who display one or more of the following traits:

a resistance to change, eagerness to shift blame onto someone else and a feeling of being a victim when something goes wrong in the office.

2. **Make negative people aware.** Many times, a negative-thinking office worker may not even know they are spreading less-than-positive vibes through an office. Tactfully approach the person about the situation, pointing out the adverse affect they are having on co-workers.

3. **Find a hidden talent.** Instead of continually focusing on a person's negative attitude, try to find the positive things that the person brings to your office. Perhaps they have the ability, when properly motivated, to work quickly. Try to persuade the negative thinker to carry over their positive approach to all aspects of their job performance. A positive outlook can be just as strong of an influence as a negative one.

4. **Create reminders.** At times, even if they're making a true effort to be more positive, negative-thinking office workers can still fall back on old habits, casting a dark cloud and reducing overall office productivity. Establish a process whereby each time negativity enters the equation, a reminder to be positive is executed. For instance, perhaps each time a negative word is uttered, a small amount of money (a nickel or dime) is put into a kitty that at some point can be used to help fund an office party.

Dear Sharon:

I work in a small law firm where things seem to be divided in two. One partner and their employees, and the other partner and those employees. The problem lies in that one of those employees likes to start conflict and is an uncontrollable gossip who will start in on anything, even if she has to invent it. She is way too bitter, but we can't say anything to her boss, because the two women are friends. It's unbearable! Please help!

Nancy, Legal Secretary

Dear Nancy,

Try ignoring the conflict starter. One of the reasons she sounds off could be that she enjoys getting a reaction from her co-workers. If that strategy doesn't work, don't be afraid to confront her (calmly) and tell her you don't like her behavior. If that still doesn't work, take things to a higher court and arrange a meeting to quietly discuss the situation with both law partners.

More, from Less

Corporate downsizing can be challenging; here are five ways to get more done with fewer people.

At times, some companies tend to cut back on their staffs. This forces department heads in all kinds of companies, perhaps yours, to find ways in which to finish their projects and meet their deadlines just as they always have—albeit with fewer people to get the job done. If ever you needed a reason to get your ACT together, this is it.

Here are five ideas to help you address the current crunch and do more, with less:

1. **Plan ahead.** Certainly not all projects can be planned to the most intricate detail—in fact many seem to fall from the sky when least expected. However, with projects you know are on the horizon, be sure to set up a timetable, a list of responsibilities for who will do what, and, most important, stick to your plan as the project proceeds in order to remain on schedule. You know how strongly I feel about writing down timelines and goals. I can't stress it enough.

2. **Focus on strengths.** If you're a team leader, you probably already know who on your team is best at doing what. In tackling a project, be sure to assign tasks accordingly. For instance, if your department is creating a research study

and one team member is strongest in gathering the data itself, be sure they do that task. If on the other hand, someone else is stronger at actually writing the study, assign that responsibility to them.

3. **Avoid conflicts.** As in any endeavor that requires cooperation, an efficiently run office is dependent upon everyone getting along and working together. Personal conflicts, particularly when people are already stretched to the limit, will almost always cause setbacks in getting work completed. Avoid these conflicts by addressing them immediately, right at the first sign of a problem, before things have a chance to escalate.

4. **Offer rewards.** This is not bribery, it's just a smart business approach that many successful bosses take. Getting a pared-down staff to perform beyond their capabilities might be a simple matter of taking the team out to lunch once in a while.

5. **Be realistic.** Everyone wants to be a hero, and, of course, a small amount of fear may enter into the equation if your company is downsizing. Yet, neither of these factors should mean that you and your department can work beyond human limitations. If a deadline or the workload of a particular project seems utterly unrealistic, discuss the situation with your supervisor to at least see if it's possible to work something out. It's better to be up front than not make the deadline.

Micro Management

Got a big office project? Break it down into small steps and things will go smoother.

The temptation to tackle demanding projects in the office with full force, trying to get as much done as you can in a single attempt, is common to many people. While deadlines are usually a consideration in a hectic office, and a "superhero" or "all or nothing" approach may work sometimes, chances are an office project will proceed more efficiently (and probably more quickly) if you tackle individual pieces of the project step by step, instead of attempting to swallow the entire project in a single gulp.

Here are some straightforward suggestions:

1. **Make a list and refer to it often.** Let's say that your boss has asked you to rearrange the customer invoice file, going back a full five years to re-file everything by the type of project rather than by customer name in which the file is currently arranged. Instead of going about the project haphazardly, you should proceed in small and logical steps. For instance, you must first determine each type of project that you will eventually file. You must create new tab headings for your newly arranged files, remove documents from the file and then put them back into the file in your new arrangement. Plus, depending on

your specific recordkeeping needs, there may be countless other details you need to address in order to complete the project. Before beginning the project, think everything out, then write down the procedural steps on a piece of paper—giving you a written blueprint to follow.

2. **Create a timetable.** Even if your boss has not given you a deadline to complete the re-filing project mentioned above, you don't want the project to linger because that will reflect negatively on your abilities to manage the job. For each of the steps you write down in the list described above, also assign a date for each step to be completed. As I mention often, having a visible timetable to work from will allow you to remain better focused on the individual tasks that will eventually lead to completion of the project.

3. **Stay on schedule and cross things off your list.** Falling behind in your timetable may force you to rush later on, and that can mean mistakes. Once you designate a time frame that shows when each step in your project must be completed, stick to it. What's more, as you finish each step, cross it off the list. This will help you keep the project moving forward, and it will also give you a sense of accomplishment.

4. **Avoid procrastination.** When you find yourself overwhelmed and you just can't get started, try allocating ten minutes to the project. Chances are once you start you will actually finish.

Of course, there are many other strategies you may think of to help a project proceed more smoothly. The important thing to remember though is that by "micro managing" the project a piece at a time and chipping away at it little by little, you will remove a lot of the stress associated with a demanding office project and you will actually be more organized—and more effective—in your approach!

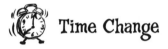 **Time Change**

How to shift valuable minutes from less important office tasks to priority ones.

With so much to do every day in your office, how do you get it all done—particularly when there are so many time-consuming "little jobs" and details to worry about?

Here are three simple, yet effective, strategies for going about office tasks so that you can devote more time to bigger projects and less time to smaller ones:

1. **Have a game plan.** Obviously, the creation of a large presentation for your boss will take more time than other things that may be part of your job description, such as typing a memo. Let's say you have three days to complete the presentation and you estimate that the project will take a total of twelve hours. Plan to devote a full four hours each day to the presentation and resist the

temptation to divert from your plan by doing other things during that time, including typing the memo.

2. **Stick to your guns.** No one expects you to be a machine, not even your boss. If your supervisor has given you a large project to complete, such as revamping three years' worth of your company's customer files in a matter of one week, be sure that the boss is aware that this project needs to be given priority status. If the boss tries to also drop a whole bunch of other little projects on you, such as addressing envelopes, remind your supervisor that in order to meet the big project deadline, you need to devote your time and resources now. You may be surprised at how understanding the boss will be, especially if he or she really needs the big project completed in just one week. Present all of your projects to your boss and ask which one he or she needs first.

3. **Pick your spots.** Studies have proven that the majority of people who work in offices are most productive during the early part of a given day. If you have a large, demanding project—such as the development of a highly detailed proposal for your department—try to attack that project during the morning hours when you will probably have the most energy. Save the afternoon hours, when your mind and body will naturally be winding down, for more mundane tasks like organizing the office supply closet or, as I mentioned before, filing.

Minute by Minute

Easy ways to save valuable time on five common office tasks.

Most people don't realize it, but, with all the tasks you perform every day in the office, you may be wasting several minutes simply by not performing those tasks most efficiently. Fact is, the time you may be wasting could otherwise be put to better use. Furthermore, you might not realize that the unnecessary minutes you're spending can quickly add up to hours of unproductive time each week!

Here are some easy suggestions for saving valuable time on five tasks that are common to just about everyone who works in an office:

1. **Use macros to automate word processing functions.** As mentioned before in this guide, things you do over and over in a document such as indenting paragraphs in a certain way, assigning bold or italic to names that are used in the document again and again, or creating headings for your pages—as well as a myriad of other functions—can all be performed in a fraction of the time by assigning macros to automate those functions. For details about using macros to save time on repetitive word processing tasks, consult your software's documentation.

2. **E-mail instead of writing paper memos.** It's much faster,

and more environmentally friendly, to simply click a memo to a co-worker rather than go to the trouble of physically putting the information down on paper then arranging for the memo to be routed.

3. **Use color in your files.** I've talked about the value of color many times in this book. Here's a reminder of how vital using color folders can be: Studies have shown that color coding your files can reduce the amount of time it takes to find specific papers by 33 percent or more.

4. **Maintain a neat desk.** Obviously, as I mention so often, a messy desk can be a real time stealer. Think about it, how many times have you wasted several minutes searching for a "missing" document that was buried the whole time under a pile of papers? Sure, it's not easy to keep your desk neat when you get especially busy, but making the effort to do so can really pay off in time efficiency!

5. **Write things down.** You might be amazed how many people go about their business day with absolutely no plan in place. Often, they spend many minutes each day just trying to gather their thoughts and remember the next task they need to complete. Solution? Spend a few moments making a list and you'll be rewarded in the long run with less downtime.

Homeward Bound

Want to leave the office on time tonight?
Here are four things to avoid.

You're dedicated to your job, and sometimes working extra hours is necessary and you're glad to pitch in. However, most nights you want to be able to finish for the day on time and get home. Problem is, for many office professionals there's often something that disrupts you at the end of the day, causing you to stay past your normal working hours.

Here are four situations to try and avoid as quitting time draws near:

1. **Last-minute phone calls.** You've experienced it, the call at 5:00 that lasts until 5:30. Of course, answering the call no matter what time may be required depending on your job description. But if it's not and your scheduled hours are until 5:00, it's okay to let voice mail take the call so you can leave on time.

2. **The talkative end-of-day visitor.** You know this person, that co-worker who doesn't care about going home on time and often stops by your desk as you're packing up for the day and ends up chatting for forty-five minutes. If you need (or want) to leave for the day, simply explain in a polite but firm way that you must be going. They'll understand.

3. **The mid-strife crises.** Many times in the office, you'll find yourself in the midst of a pressure-packed project under a tight deadline. As the end of the day gets closer, all your project materials are scattered about, however you need to tidy up your workspace before leaving. When you're extra busy, make a conscious effort to be aware of the clock, and schedule your daily project cleanup as part of the day's activities, allowing enough minutes to finish while still being able to depart the office on time.

4. **Taking on too much.** You're ambitious and you want the boss to know you deserve that big promotion. Sometimes though, people have a tendency to accept more work than they can handle and things snowball until they never seem to be able to go home on time. If this is the case, perhaps a discussion with your boss might be the solution. He or she may not even realize that you're overloaded.

CHAPTER 6

DEALING WITH YOUR BOSS

Keeping It All in Perspective

No man is an island and we all have someone at some point we need to be accountable to whether at work, school or at home. At work he or she can be a real taskmaster at times, demanding more and more from you, especially during times when companies are cutting back on staff and asking more from their employees. Or, perhaps you simply don't see eye to eye on some topics. We're talking about your boss or someone you have to answer to; the relationship you have with that person can make a big difference in how much you enjoy your job and also the opportunities you have to move up the company ladder. This chapter has some tips you'll find most helpful.

Mind over Manager

How to handle a cranky boss.

All right, so your supervisor acts like a jerk sometimes. Before you do something crazy like stick your boss's head in a laser printer, read on—there are ways you can handle the situation and make it work to *your* advantage.

First of all, you need to keep an open mind. Remember that your boss is probably under considerable pressure from his or her boss and much of that pressure can filter through to you. Just because the person you report to is always in a bad mood, it doesn't mean he or she is a bad person.

Here are some practical approaches for dealing with your boss's swinging moods:

1. **Open the lines of communication.** Don't be afraid to ask your boss what's wrong. Chances are, he or she is just waiting to vent a little frustration with someone who will listen. Also, this will give you an opportunity to find out if there is anything you are doing, or not doing, that is irritating your boss.

2. **Stay one step ahead.** One of the best ways to keep bosses happy is to take the initiative yourself and anticipate their needs. For example, even if you're not asked to set up a better routing system for interoffice memos, do it anyway—and let your boss know so you get the credit you deserve.

3. **Be good at what you do.** Obviously, if your boss is easily

upset, you don't want to rock the boat further. So always get to work on time, complete your assignments on schedule and don't be a complainer—this will only antagonize your boss.

4. **Take a breather.** Once in a while, if your boss is in a particularly nasty state of mind, you may need to clear the air—literally. If possible at lunchtime, go for a walk and get some fresh air; you'll be surprised how your own tolerance level will improve when you come back to the office.

5. **If all else fails, consider your options.** Even if you try each of the above approaches, the situation may still seem hopeless because your boss's bad moods are just too much to endure day in and day out. If this is the case, it may be a good idea to discreetly pursue opportunities in other departments within your company.

Above all, remain patient and nonconfrontational. Snapping back at a cranky boss will only make matters worse.

No, No, a Thousand Times No

It's okay to say "nay" when the boss overloads you with work.

Ever feel like you're being dumped on? You're not alone. Millions of people in offices around the world complain about the same thing. However, everyone reaches a point where they simply can't handle any more work. At that point, according to management experts, it's all right to explain to your boss that you're maxed out.

In fact, a recent poll of one hundred supervisors showed that many bosses don't even realize that their team members may be overloaded with work, and when a team member states that he or she has a full plate, the boss is likely to assign the work to someone else. Best of all, the boss actually appreciates the honesty of someone who admits they've temporarily reached their limit.

Remember, the boss's priorities are to get the job done right and get it done on time. If accomplishing those goals means getting help for you, the experts agree that your boss will probably do so without feeling any less confident in your abilities.

So, if you feel yourself becoming overworked to the breaking point, just say so. But don't forget to consider some obvious words of caution: It's probably a good idea to not overdo it when saying no. In other words, don't get into a constant habit of telling your boss you can't handle any more assignments. In addition, watch your timing when saying no (for example, right before your annual review is probably not the best time to ask your boss to find another dumpee).

Dear Sharon:

Hi, Sharon! First of all, I want to say I really enjoy the I Hate Filing Newsletter! The topics are very pertinent and the tips are immediately useful. My question is: How can I best explain to our admin assistant the importance of keeping the filing caught up? I've tried explaining that it's much easier for her and the rest of us to find things if they're filed promptly, and that the task of filing is not so overwhelming if it doesn't pile up, but so far this hasn't been effective. Any additional ideas? Thank you!

Leanna, Office Manager

Dear Leanna,

Perhaps your approach should be one that never fails in most business situations: emphasize the bottom line! In a recent article in this newsletter entitled "The Color of Money," we explained that filing efficiently often can save a company substantial operating costs—both immediately and over time. Explain to the administrative assistant that getting behind in the filing can cause lapses in productivity, which can adversely affect the profitability of a company, which ultimately will mean lower raises for herself and everyone else. Speaking directly to someone's wallet will usually do the trick!

Barbarians at the Gate

Ways to protect your boss from obnoxiously persistent callers.

Perhaps part of your job duties involves answering phone calls to your boss's office. Inevitably, your boss will ask you to put certain callers through and "take a message" from others.

Problem is, the callers who don't get through will usually keep trying, again and again—even if you make it clear that your boss does not ever want to speak to them. What do you do? Here are some tips:

1. **Ask for credentials.** Explain to the caller that your company does not accept unsolicited phone calls. Request that the caller send information instead, perhaps some literature about their company, and if your boss is interested, he or she will get back to the caller. This may not deter the caller completely, but it will put them off at least for a while.

2. **Accept the call yourself.** Put the responsibility for handling the call in your own hands, by stating to the caller that the "buck stops with me," and you will be glad to answer any questions the caller may have.

3. **Stay away from excuses.** Avoid the natural temptation to "make something up," such as saying the boss is busy at the moment or on vacation. This will only make the caller

more determined to get through, and put you in the awkward position of possibly having to explain a lie later on.

4. **May the force be with you.** Above all, do not be tentative with the caller. When you tell them that the boss does not wish to take their call, it's likely they won't want to take "no" for an answer. As always, you still need to be polite and civil, however, you must be forceful in firmly stating that the boss will not accept the call.

Change at the Top

Strategies for adjusting to life in the office when a new boss takes over.

Perhaps you have worked for the same boss for several years. Or, perhaps the management in your office sometimes seems like a "revolving door" where the people in charge can change as often as the weather. Either way, adjustments need to be made whenever a new boss assumes the reins of responsibilities, and it doesn't matter if the new boss comes from another company or has been promoted from within.

Here are some straightforward tips to help make the transition smoother, both for you and for your new boss:

1. **Have a "sit down" right away.** Communication is one of the most important aspects of getting off to a successful start with a new boss. Chances are, your new supervisor

will take the initiative and arrange a "get to know each other" meeting. However, if they don't, you should suggest a meeting as a way of opening up the doors of two-way communication.

2. **Learn what's expected of you.** Even if you've been in your present job position for many years, it's possible (even likely) that your new boss will have a few expectations of you and your co-workers that may differ from your previous boss's expectations. Don't hesitate to ask what those expectations are. After all, you're not a mind reader.

3. **Remain positive in the face of change.** Remember that change is never easy, not for you, your co-workers or your new boss. Yes, you'll all have to work a little harder making adjustments while getting used to the new chain of command, but avoid appearing as though the transition is annoying you—this will label you as a negative team member and could thwart your opportunities for promotions later on. Change may actually bring you opportunities you didn't have before.

4. **Avoid comparisons.** Probably the last thing your new boss wants to hear is how your old boss did things. Remember that the new person in charge wants to make her or his own mark, so keep an open mind and resist the temptation to compare the two in terms of "good points" and "bad points."

5. **Give it time.** Like almost everything else in life, a transition to a new supervisor takes time to work itself out. Yes,

things could get awkward at the beginning of the transition, but remain patient and before you know it you'll likely develop a rewarding working relationship with your new boss that eventually will benefit you both.

Dear Sharon:

I have a new boss (a female vice president). Because she is new to the company, she has been having many, many meetings, trying to meet people, gain knowledge about the company, etc. It has been a real challenge to keep track of all the meetings and make sure they all take place. Here is the real problem: She is constantly late for her meetings or cancels them at the last minute. I know this is not a reflection on me, but in being conscientious, I feel responsible! I can't help but feel that after awhile, she will lose her credibility with others because she keeps canceling or arriving late to her meetings. Do you have advice for me as her administrative assistant to try to keep face with others?

Laura, Administrative Assistant

Dear Laura,

First of all, because your boss is new to the company, you should give her a little leeway in adjusting to her new job. She's probably inundated with things to do right now and may in fact be forgetting about the meetings. Try providing reminders either by telling her personally, or typing up a meeting schedule each day in advance—then follow up to remind her to keep on schedule. If your company has e-mail, you can also send her electronic reminders. The bottom line is, part of your job responsibility as your boss's assistant is to help make sure she keeps her appointments. In doing so, you will help make yourself invaluable to her.

Role Reversal

Your boss has been demoted, you've been promoted—here's how to handle it.

Talk about being in a tough spot. Maybe you've reported to your boss for ten years. Now, due to a change in management strategy, everything has been reversed and you're the boss—while your former boss now reports to you!

Phew! As you might expect, this scenario could certainly be dicey. Here are some approaches that may help you handle the situation.

1. **Have a conversation, immediately.** You know the new reporting arrangement could create some chilly relations between you and your former boss, and he or she knows it too. So talk about it, get things out in the open. And come to an understanding that you're both going to be professional about it and leave any animosity out of the equation.

2. **Take the high road.** The last thing your former boss needs is for you to gloat about your new promotion. Obviously, that could just add fuel to what could be a simmering fire. Accept your new position with grace and dignity, and even if you've had some serious differences with your former boss in the past, avoid the temptation to utilize your newfound power to settle those differences.

3. **Be yourself.** You were promoted for a reason, you deserve it because you've worked hard and done a great job. Therefore, don't try to be someone you're not just because you may feel uncomfortable with your ex-boss as your assistant.

Communication Breakthroughs

Five strategies for communicating better with your boss.

Ever feel like your supervisor is speaking a foreign language? Well, communication is a two-way street and it's possible that your boss feels the same way about your abilities to express yourself.

The following are five tips for breaking through the communication barrier that can sometimes exist between employees and the people they report to:

1. **Pay attention.** All too often, a conversation between a supervisor and a team member gets cluttered with distractions. Perhaps while your boss is explaining a new project to you, instead of listening carefully to what's being said, you're wondering "How will I get the project completed on time?" Or, instead of absorbing the boss's ideas for a new procedure in your department, you're thinking about how your co-workers will accept the new approach. The bottom line? Listen carefully, understand fully.

2. **Ask questions.** Many people are intimidated or even afraid to ask their boss about something because they fear that the boss will perceive them as someone who simply doesn't understand. This is not true. Almost all bosses

will be pleased when you ask questions, for several reasons. First, it demonstrates that you want to be absolutely certain about what is being communicated; second, it shows that you're eager to learn more; and third, it opens the door for two-way communication and a healthy exchange of ideas.

3. **Write things down.** If you become involved in a lengthy meeting with your boss, it may be nearly impossible to remember everything that is said. Do not hesitate to take notes in order to be sure that you clearly and accurately receive and remember what is being discussed.

4. **Make suggestions.** Sometimes, your boss will just want you to listen to what he or she is saying. However, most times your boss will be pleased to hear your opinion on a particular subject. Be careful not to contradict the boss or openly correct what he or she is saying in front of fellow workers, but go ahead and state your opinions if you feel they are good ones—the boss will appreciate your abilities to think on your own.

5. **Follow up later.** In many circumstances, conversations with your boss will be over and done with. Yet, at other times, particularly if the meeting is lengthy and involves intricate details, it might be a good idea a few days later to report back to your supervisor just to say something like "With regard to that idea you had for a new filing system, I'm working on it right now and will have it completed by Thursday," or, "I thought further about your plan for a

new invoicing procedure and I have the following ideas of my own." Following up demonstrates that you are being proactive about what you and your boss discussed and that you are enthusiastically implementing what the boss has said.

Let me share a personal lesson that was taught to me early in my working career. I was working for the vice president of sales. He was difficult and demanding and at one point I didn't think I could continue working for him. In a private conversation with the sales manager, I learned a valuable lesson that has helped me through the years. He told me to look for one positive attribute in this person and concentrate on that. I found that my boss had a great sense of humor. I took the manager's advice and was able to turn a negative into a positive. It's amazing what a little bit of humor can do.

Dear Sharon:

I need some input as to how a supervisor should handle an employee who is late, takes long breaks and lunches and has no sick or leave time accumulated, [yet is] constantly sick or on leave. What would be the correct way to approach this person? Thank you. I love your newsletter.

Ivette

Dear Ivette,

Thanks for the compliment about our newsletter! As someone who has managed associates for many years and encountered all kinds of situations similar to the one you describe, I would first and foremost recommend a good and thorough talk with the employee; however, be careful to keep the meeting nonconfrontational. It's possible the employee might not even realize they are sidestepping the rules that all employees must abide by. On the other hand, perhaps they are testing you, seeing how much they can get away with. Point out that it is not just you, but the company itself that dictates that employees must arrive on schedule, and that employees must also take breaks and lunches within specific time frames, and not abuse sick leave privileges. However, keep in mind that the employee could have some sort of medical problem, or possibly a personal one. If that is the case, you may want to refer the dilemma to your company's Human Resources department and let them take appropriate action on the matter.

CHAPTER 7

INTERACTING
WITH CO-WORKERS

Maintaining Peace and Harmony

We all interact with co-workers, whether it is in a large or home office, or working with individuals who help get personal projects accomplished. These rules apply to all, but especially to those of us in office situations. Working in a busy, hectic and often crowded office can present many challenges. Maybe the biggest one is successfully getting along with all the different personalities that typically make up a business office. From dealing with "cube-mates" to navigating the tricky world of office politics, here are some ideas for you to consider.

Your Space or Mine?

Four ways to claim your territory in a crowded office.

With available office space at a premium these days, and costs per square foot skyrocketing, it seems that many companies are cramming their employees into working areas that don't allow much room for each person.

Of course, if you aren't lucky enough to have your own office  with four actual walls and a door, working in cramped quarters every day can create a feeling that your co-workers are literally on top of you. And at times, you can even feel as though inconsiderate co-workers are "trespassing" on your workspace. So how do you make sure that the little space you've been allotted remains yours and yours alone? Here are a few tips and reminders:

1. **Create boundaries.** Many offices are arranged with dividers separating workers, in what is known as a "bull pen" configuration. If you have dividers separating your workspace from that of your co-workers, you may have all the privacy you need. However, if your desk is located in an open space, it may be a good idea (if possible) to try and set up items around your desk that will provide boundaries—such as a bookcase or a large plant that will provide some privacy.

2. **Build "walls."** Another idea for "sectioning off" your workspace and creating some privacy for yourself is to line the edges of your desk with such things as in/out trays, binders or books. These items will effectively provide a wall-like effect that will make it easier for you to concentrate on your work.

3. **Make your mark.** Sometimes, especially if your desk is positioned in a well-traveled area of your office, co-workers may view your workspace as a "community" working area and plop themselves down to make a call or use your computer. Be sure to put a nameplate that clearly identifies your work area as yours, and don't be afraid to remind co-workers that your workspace belongs to you.

4. **Get personal.** Another good way to let co-workers know that your workspace is indeed your own is to place photos of your relatives and friends throughout your work area (provided that your company allows personal photos in the office). As with a nameplate, this clearly designates your working area as your own personal space. However, don't use too many personal items as this could cause clutter.

Dear Sharon:

My co-workers and I are arranged in one room with cubicle walls as the only separation. One of my co-workers is always sick. But, from the first day that she started working here, over a year ago, she constantly clears her throat—very loudly. This occurs about every thirty seconds ALL DAY LONG, EVERY DAY. I try to tune it out, but it's very difficult. I know she suffers from allergies, but some days I almost go insane from the constant "noise." I used to think I was a horrible person because of this, but I found out that EVERYONE is annoyed by it and almost to the same point that I am. Is there anything we can do?

Stressed out from noise

Dear Stressed,

First and foremost, it must be kept in mind that this person has a medical condition. Certainly, the noise must be annoying, but do not confront the person over the situation as this could create resentment and possible legal implications. Consult privately with your supervisor, and perhaps an arrangement can be made to have the person moved to another location within your office where the noise won't be so distracting.

Thanks, but No Thanks

How to say no when co-workers constantly ask you for donations or try to sell you something.

Sometimes, working in an office can be downright expensive. The people you work with, although they usually mean well, can put a serious drain on your pocketbook by continually approaching you for money to be used toward some sort of worthy cause.

Obviously, no one can afford to give away money all the time. After all, you work hard for your paycheck and you have plenty of personal expenses to worry about. But do take into consideration whether you have been selling for your own causes. This can put you in a vulnerable position when it is time for payback. I myself have sold my share of candy and wrapping paper.

Here are a few suggestions for dealing with a steady stream of co-workers who approach you with their hands out:

1. **Remember that honesty is the best policy.** Certainly, there are plenty of important causes that are indeed worthy of donations, including many charities. However, that doesn't mean you always have to contribute to them. If a co-worker asks for money toward one of these causes, it's okay to politely explain that you simply cannot afford to give any money at this time. Believe it or not, your co-worker will understand.

2. **Be choosey.** Establish your own guidelines concerning

those cases in which you will fork over some cash and those in which you won't—and stick to your guidelines. For example, you might always contribute to the cost of a celebration party for any co-workers who've recently been promoted in your department, but you will not contribute for workers outside your department. In time, your fellow employees will get to know your guidelines, and they will not only adhere to them, they will actually respect you for them.

3. **Have a ready excuse.** It's very common for people to help their kids out by selling things (such as Girl Scout cookies) among co-workers. Problem is, the costs of these purchases can really add up. Be prepared to offer a viable reason why you cannot afford to buy the cookies; for instance, your own child is also selling cookies and you have already bought five boxes of them. Or, perhaps your co-worker wants a donation for their church. Explain that you contribute to your own church every week and making another contribution is not in your budget.

Politically Correct

How to make office politics work for you.

You know the type. The "political animal" who has an office down the hall from you, the person who always seems to be working an angle—or somebody. Unfortunately (or fortunately, depending on how you look at it), office politics are a way of life in companies large and small. Your company is probably no exception.

So what do you do? How can you use office politics to your own advantage?

Here are a few ideas:

1. **Get visible.** Opportunities that can be "politically charged" are likely to happen at any time. Perhaps the boss is forming a steering committee to investigate ways to make your entire company more productive. Volunteering for such a visible committee would create great exposure for you.

2. **Know who your friends are (and aren't).** Be continually aware of co-workers who may be trying to look good in the boss's eye at your expense—for example, someone may try to take credit for ideas that are yours. At the same time, people at levels above your position can become allies who could eventually help with the advancement of your career, so nurture these kinds of relationships.

3. **Never take sides.** If a dispute arises in your office, be extra careful not to become opinionated about who is right or wrong. You never know how such an opinion may come back to haunt you.

4. **Make yourself available.** If your boss asks you to attend a business luncheon, or a social event such as a party for

a co-worker, don't hesitate to say "Yes, I'll be there." Such an occasion could provide a great forum to let your real personality shine through, as well as establish new contacts.

5. **Become a versatile performer.** Be eager to demonstrate to your boss all the things you can do on the job. For example, maybe your actual job description only requires that you file and answer phones. Show the boss that you can also create a presentation on your computer. This will enhance your value to the company.

Dear Sharon:

We have a woman in our department who put in her resignation, worked her two-week notice, had her going-away party, etc. She has been helping out a few hours a week since she "quit." Now she doesn't like her new job and wants to come back to our department. Someone has already been hired to take her place. She doesn't want the job that is available on second shift. This has caused a lot of hard feelings in the department. What should we do? What should we tell her?

Christine, Medical Records

Dear Christine,

Unless you are the person who runs the department, I think you should tell her nothing. This is a matter for the department supervisor to decide. The first thing for the supervisor to consider is the sincerity of the person in wanting to return to her old job. After all, she has already "cried wolf" by stating her desire to leave then changing her mind. Secondly, it must be determined how valuable and/or necessary the person is to the department now that someone else has filled the position. Once these things are carefully considered, then a decision can be made, but the decision must be addressed by the person in charge.

War and Peace

Tips for settling an office dispute.

We've all witnessed it. Two people disagree in the office, usually over something silly like whose turn it is to make the coffee. And suddenly, World War III breaks out. Sometimes, the best policy is to not get involved. Many times, you have no choice.

If, for example, you are responsible for supervising the people who are disputing, you simply have to intercede, quickly, before the warring parties kill each other!

Here are some common-sense strategies for addressing a dispute in your office:

1. **Assess the damage.** Avoid a sudden knee-jerk reaction when two or more co-workers become involved in a quarrel. Step back (if just for a few moments) and objectively figure out exactly what is going on.

2. **Protect the innocent.** Do not involve workers in your office who have nothing to do with the dispute. Resist the urge to solicit opinions from bystanders, because this will only prompt other people to join the fray, which in turn will cause the "war" to escalate.

3. **Arrange a summit.** Talking things out is perhaps the best way to settle any dispute. Allow both parties to speak their minds, calmly. Chances are, just clearing the air will diffuse the situation.

4. **Remain neutral.** Be careful not to take sides when co-workers have a disagreement. This will surely create enemies for you and will also undermine your ability to act as a mediator in settling the confrontation.

5. **Come to terms.** Once you've heard both sides of the scenario, be sure that a clear and concise conclusion is brought to the table. In other words, make certain that each participant understands precisely what his or her role is in ending the dispute.

Dear Sharon:

I have a suggestion [for the lady with the messy colleagues] that worked for us. We have a "coffee club." To avoid one person getting stuck cleaning up, we post a schedule. Each person is responsible for one week and we rotate. A gentle reminder at the beginning of the week serves to solve any misunderstandings. If that person forgets, the pot remains dirty until the next day when it is that person's responsibility to make the coffee. Therefore, they very rarely forget! Hope this helps someone else in a "messy" situation.

Rose Ann, School Secretary

Dear Rose Ann,

Thanks so much for your great suggestion. (As many readers may recall, I recently received a letter from a frustrated person who was dealing with co-workers who never cleaned up after themselves in the lunchroom and around the coffee station—leaving a constant mess for someone else to clean.) Pat, I love it when thoughtful people like you take the time to share their ideas about life in the office with our fellow readers. I'm sure there are lots of other readers out there with all kinds of ways to enhance office life, so drop me an e-mail!! Remember, this an open forum, and we welcome any comments, feedback or thoughts that anyone may have.

Rallying the Troops

How to get co-workers to pull together when a big project arises.

Imagine this scenario: The most important customer presentation of the year is fast approaching, and you're in charge of preparing your department to put its best foot forward. It's a project that will take a well-coordinated effort involving everyone in your office. There's no time for mistakes, and you need the commitment of each member of your office team to make the presentation the best it can be.

The following are some simple ways to ensure that you get everybody pulling in the same direction in order to complete the project successfully.

1. **Plan your approach.** Before beginning the project, decide exactly what needs to be accomplished and who will accomplish it.

2. **Establish a schedule.** It's always a good idea to have a timeline that everyone in the office can refer to. Having a visual record of project tasks and due dates gives your entire team something concrete they can work toward.

3. **Assign responsibilities.** Gather everyone in the same room and carefully explain to each person exactly what their role is in completing the project. You might even want to write down a short description for each

co-worker, outlining the specific duties they will need to perform in order to get the project finished on time.

4. **Check status regularly.** At least every week, and at shorter intervals if your timeline demands, have everyone involved with the project meet to discuss how things are proceeding. This will make it much easier for you to address potential issues before they become roadblocks to finishing the project within your time frame.

5. **Give incentives.** If you're in a position to do so, offer possible rewards to your team that will help motivate them to work harder and faster. It doesn't have to be a big thing, just something that lets them know you appreciate their efforts, such as extra break times when parts of the project are completed, or perhaps the opportunity to go home fifteen minutes early.

6. **Pour on the gravy.** Obviously, what you and everyone on your team is working toward is a successful outcome to your project. When that outcome happens, be sure to thank your team and tell them how great everything turned out. This will not only give them a sense of satisfaction, but it will also help make them eager to tackle the next project when it arises.

Dear Sharon,

I became a temp three years ago and have been working full time for most of that time. I am sixty-three and owned and operated a factory in Chicago for thirty years. I have no problem being a clerk; it is challenging and keeps me busy and, more important, pays the bills. My question is: How can I maintain good supervisor and fellow employee relations without socializing? I am always friendly and helpful but have no desire to socialize.

Eldon, Data Base Manager

Dear Eldon,

We answer all kinds of questions here, not just "filing-related" but also questions about how to make relationships with co-workers more pleasant and more rewarding. My suggestion: meet your fellow employees halfway. You don't need to socialize with them after work; however, once in a while it might be a good idea to extend your "working" environment beyond the office itself, perhaps by going to lunch together at a local restaurant, or organizing some kind of activity during break time such as a friendly game of cards in the cafeteria. Your point about maintaining a "good supervisor" relationship is well-taken. Many bosses are hesitant to get too close to their team members on a "friendship" level for fear of compromising the ability to supervise. However, it has also been shown in several studies that workers respond very favorably (and many times work harder and more diligently) when the boss takes the time and makes the effort to occasionally interact with them on a personal basis.

Double Trouble?

You've been teamed with a co-worker and it's not working out. Here's what to do.

Perhaps it's a conflict of different personalities. Maybe you can't seem to see eye to eye on what should be the proper order of steps for completing an office project. Or maybe you simply disagree overall.

Yet, you've been asked by your supervisor to work together and finish the project by the end of next week, so it's probably a good idea to put aside your differences and work through them. Here are some suggestions:

1. **Lose the attitude.** Showing your dislike for someone you're working closely with will only add fuel to an already potentially combustible situation. Be professional, and do your best not to speak to your co-worker in an unfriendly, threatening or condescending way.

2. **Concentrate on the prize.** Even if you and your co-worker do not agree on most things, you probably do have one goal in common: to complete the project on time in the best way possible and please the boss. So when the air gets unusually tense between you and your project partner, try to focus your attention on what needs to be achieved instead of what is annoying you about the other person.

3. **If necessary, consider some diplomacy.** Granted, your co-worker may be entirely unreasonable when it comes to agreeing with you on some points. However, it's likely you have some aspect of your lives that the two of you can relate to, perhaps it's a love of gardening, or sports or a certain movie. World leaders as well as executives at the highest levels have "broken the ice" and opened up new avenues of successful communication by simply finding something to talk about that is of interest to both parties.

4. **Compromise whenever possible.** Nobody can have absolutely everything their own way. Yes, your co-worker may be the most stubborn person in the world and unwilling to budge on some differences, but he or she may well be willing to accept your approach on others. So win a few, lose a few; in the long run you may discover that making compromises can go a long way in satisfying your needs as well as those of your co-worker.

Dear Sharon:

[My co-worker] sits behind me and always wants me to fax things for her and wants me to help her do her work. What should I say to her as our supervisor is in charge and expects each one of us to do our own work? Thanks for reading this.

Grace, Insurance Correspondent

Dear Grace,

I do not know exactly what your relationship is with your co-worker, but it appears that she's taking advantage of you. Tell her, politely but in no uncertain terms, that you are very busy with the work that has been assigned to you and you do not have time to do her work in addition to yours. Believe it or not, she may not realize that she is imposing on you, and telling her so could solve the problem. If not, you may have to approach your supervisor and let the boss make a decision as to how to best handle the situation.

Holding Down the Fort

Your boss is going on vacation and you're in charge—now what?

Just the thought of it can be intimidating. Life in the office is going along smoothly, when suddenly, you're thrust onto center stage as the person who will rule the roost while the head honcho is off on a two-week cruise in the Caribbean.

Sure, it's a challenge, and it will certainly be a great experience for you to test your management skills as the temporary boss. However, where do you start? How do you smoothly go from co-worker to manager, literally overnight?

Here are some simple suggestions for beginning your reign as the substitute person in charge:

1. **Call a meeting, pronto.** First things first, and that means making certain that everyone in the office realizes you will be calling the shots while the department head is away. Gather the entire team for a powwow on your first morning as temporary boss, and briefly go over what's on the agenda for each person.

2. **Establish the rules.** Much like when you were in grade school, it's tempting to try and kick back a little when the real "teacher" (or, in this case, the everyday boss) is away. Keep that from happening by discussing your role and the roles of your co-workers, clearly pointing out that even though the boss is on vacation, it will be business as usual in your office.

3. **Adhere to schedules.** Perhaps the one area, more than any other, that can be affected when a boss takes time off is the timetable for completion of various projects. Be certain that project steps do not lag while you're in charge.

4. **Relax.** Trying too hard as temporary boss can quickly alienate your co-workers. Just be yourself and do not try to change the world during the short time you will be making decisions for your office. Remember too, that executives within your company may be watching your performance and considering you for future promotions,

so it's important that you keep a cool head and demonstrate your abilities to manage effectively in everyday situations.

Positive Feedback

Showing appreciation is a sure way to motivate associates and co-workers.

Everyone loves a pat on the back. In fact, many studies have shown that people are more consistently driven to perform at peak levels when they know they will be congratulated for a job well done—rather than because of the threat of being punished for doing a poor job.

Positive reinforcement is a tried and true method for getting people in your office motivated and keeping them motivated. With that in mind, perhaps nothing goes further in prompting associates and co-workers to go the extra mile than two simple words: thank you.

The following are some easy tips for saying thanks to people in your office in ways that will best show your appreciation:

1. **Put it in writing.** A handwritten "thank you" note shows someone you've taken the time to personally recognize their efforts. Written notes on colored stationery paper, versus a thank you that is sent via e-mail, are far more likely to be saved and cherished by the recipient—for

example, handwritten notes are often posted proudly on bulletin boards.

2. **Pay attention to special occasions.** Administrative Professionals Week, which occurs every April, as well as other special times during the year such as Thanksgiving, present terrific opportunities to show your appreciation to the people you work with. Coordinating your thank you's with a special occasion makes them more memorable.

3. **Be specific in your praise.** When you thank someone in your office, be sure to point out exactly why you are so pleased with their efforts. For example, you might say, "Thanks for the great job on the sales report, especially the dynamic charts you created. Your efforts made our entire department look good." Specifics make it easier for people to repeat a good job later on, while adding substance and credibility to your praise.

4. **Avoid the fluff.** There's a fine line between sincere appreciation and shallow gratitude that appears to be invented. Associates and co-workers can definitely tell the difference, so be careful to say thanks without gushing or making people feel like they're being "schmoozed."

One Bad Apple?

**A difficult team member can spoil a bunch
of people on your team—try these solutions.**

In a busy office, where everyone is continually pressured and
facing a lot of stress, the negativity of just one worker can sometimes lower the morale and the productivity of an entire team of
co-workers.

If you're in charge of a department, a team or just a small
group of employees, you'll want to nip such a situation in the
bud, before a potentially "problem employee" becomes one who
causes deadlines to be missed, and possibly, eventually leads to
some of your associates wanting to quit their jobs and move
somewhere else.

Here are some straightforward insights about handling a difficult team member:

1. **Gather the group and talk it out.** As soon as it has come
   to your attention that one employee is being overly negative, not pulling his or her weight, or otherwise dragging
   the rest of the team down, get everyone together and
   make it clear that in order to succeed as a whole, each part
   of the team must contribute and remain positive in doing
   so. Be careful not to single out the difficult employee, and,
   hopefully, he or she will get the message.

2. **If things get worse, meet one-on-one.** If, after meeting

with your entire team, the negative approach of your one difficult member continues and perhaps grows, sit down  with that employee alone. Explain, clearly and politely yet firmly, that you are aware of the problem and then enumerate exactly what you expect of the employee in order to remedy the situation. It's very possible that the person may just be seeking attention from you, and that taking the time to meet with them in a one-on-one setting could signal that you care about the employee and are willing to take the time and effort to assist them in doing their job better. By the way, it's a good idea to also document (in writing) the information exchanged during your meeting.

3. **If still no progress, involve HR.** With some difficult employees, each of the above techniques will have very little or no effect. At that point, it's probably best to make your company's Human Resources department aware of the issue. They can advise you on the company's guidelines concerning performance and the steps that can be taken in keeping with company mandates.

CHAPTER 8

BUSINESS SKILLS MADE BETTER

Staying Competitive and Up-to-Date

As you well know, the business world is very competitive and in order to succeed—gain promotions, increase your salary and grow your business—you need to keep your working skills honed. When working from a home office you have only yourself to depend on, which makes these skills even more important. To follow is a wide range of techniques covering several different areas of business skills. Mastering each can be an important contributor to your work success and how you present yourself.

The Write Stuff

How to write more effective sales letters, memos and inter-office correspondence.

Communicating effectively on paper is one of the most important things that any person in the business world can do. However, very few people do it well.

Perhaps you work for a company that sends out large numbers of proposals and sales letters, or even requests for donations on a  frequent basis, and it's your job to generate the written materials—either by writing them from scratch or editing and typing material that has been written by someone else.

The following five tips will make any sales letter more successful. The first two tips could also be applied to virtually any other type of written correspondence, including internal memos that will be routed throughout your department or company.

1. **Write as you talk.** Being conversational engages the reader and makes your words easier to understand and digest.
2. **Keep paragraphs short.** This makes your written correspondence more visually appealing at first glance, prompting the reader to read on.
3. **Pretend you're writing the letter to yourself.** Ask

yourself, if you were in the shoes of the person receiving the letter, what would motivate you to respond?

4. **Name names.** A good sales letter includes testimonials from satisfied clients, letting readers know they are in "good company" if they use your product or service.

5. **Make an offer.** Always end a sales letter by offering something of value to the reader. For example, "We look forward to hearing from you so that we may forward your free sample." An offer calls your reader to action.

If you keep each of the above tips in mind the next time you sit down at the word processor, all of your letters—as well as your memos and other inter-office correspondence—are sure to communicate your message more effectively.

Dear Sharon,

How do I go about designing and implementing a company newsletter?

Randall, Team Leader

Dear Randall,

Inter-company and inter-departmental newsletters are a great way to keep everyone you work with informed about the latest happenings in your organization. They also provide a terrific vehicle for making announcements about the accomplishments of co-workers, ensuring that people receive the recognition they deserve. At the same time, a newsletter is a way to communicate the latest initiatives of your company or department, to talk about various business strategies, and so forth. Starting up a newsletter is easy. Begin by involving your readers, circulating a memo that asks co-workers to contribute articles and other content information—once you have the content for your newsletter, you're halfway there! Be sure to ask for photographs, and include as many photos as possible in the newsletter itself. If the photos are digital, they can simply be placed into the newsletter layout. If they're photo prints, just use a desktop scanner to turn the photos into digital images that can then be put into your newsletter layout. As for designing and printing the newsletter, you can most likely do it all right in your word processing software. Many word processing packages include highly intuitive desktop publishing functions, including professionally designed "templates" that make it fast and easy to produce your own newsletter with very little design or publishing skill. For a more finished look, you may want to consult with an outside graphics/printing company. They can advise you about such things as printing in several colors, utilizing fancy papers such as coated stocks, and printing most cost effectively in large quantities.

Letter Perfect

Tips for making business letters look great every time.

A business letter is more than just a document containing a written message. It's a reflection of the person and/or the company who created the letter. That's why it's imperative that every letter you send to every business associate must not only read well, it must also look its very best.

Here are some ideas for ensuring that your business letters convey the best image and gain immediate attention from your reader:

1. **Put spaces between paragraphs.** "White space" (the part of a document not occupied by written material) is very important in a business letter. If a person receives a letter that appears too overcrowded with type, chances are the letter will be tossed aside because the reader will think: "I don't have time to read all this."

2. **Use wide margins.** As with putting spaces between paragraphs, wide page margins of at least one inch all around your typed matter will give your letter an inviting feeling of open space, making the letter more easily readable.

3. **Underline key points.** Studies prove that many people don't actually read a business letter from beginning to end. Instead, they scan the document for phrases that have

meaning to them. Things such as your most important selling message, or the "call to action" at the end of the letter,
should be underlined so they are emphasized and more
likely to be digested by the reader.

4. **Take advantage of the technology you already have.** Most
word processing programs come complete with letter templates designed by experts. With templates, the design work is
already done; all you do is slug in the contents of your letter.

Paper Primer

Six quick lessons on choosing the right paper for business desktop publishing projects.

Perhaps your job or business calls for creating business proposals, departmental reports, letters to customers and other presentation materials that you print on your desktop printer. Today's
easy-to-use, yet powerful word processing and presentation
development software allows you to produce truly stunning documents that can "wow" your reader. However, you must not
ignore one very important element in your desktop publishing
projects: the paper they're printed on.

Fact is, selecting the right paper is critical in determining the
overall image of your documents. Here are six things you should
consider:

1. **Weight.** The most common paper for computer printers

and copiers is 20 lb. weight. To lend the perception of added importance to reports and presentations, try using 24 lb. paper.

2. **Texture.** Walk into any office products retailer or stationery store and you'll see a myriad of "fine" office paper choices, including linen or cotton laid textures. These papers are perfect for letters and other correspondence sent to customers and contacts.

3. **Brightness.** Measured on a scale of 100, more brightness provides a "whiter" look, which can enhance your document's appearance tremendously.

4. **Opacity.** This is the paper's ability to prevent "show through" and it's also measured on a scale of 100.

5. **Color.** Using color paper can add impact to your document, creating another graphic element to enhance your message. For example, you might use tan paper with dark blue ink generated from your ink-jet printer. This combination is highly pleasing to the eye and has a look of refined quality.

6. **Coating.** In addition to a choice of each of the above paper characteristics, most stationery retailers also offer shiny, coated paper for use with computer printers. Depending on the quality of your printer, the look created by these papers can rival commercial print jobs.

In all cases when choosing paper, consult your printer or copier manual to assure you select a paper that will work well with your model and not cause jams or equipment damage.

Pushing the Envelope

Want to make sure important office letters get opened? Try this technique.

For many business and office professionals, part of their responsibilities will often include preparing mailings that can be critical to the success of their companies.

In many cases, these mailings involve highly vital correspondence directed toward important customers and prospects. It's imperative that the envelopes and letters addressed to current as well as future customers not only reach the desks of their intended targets, but also get opened and read by the recipient.

Problem is, most people are overwhelmed with a constant barrage of mail, and many letters get lost in the shuffle and are completely ignored.

However, there is something you can do about that dilemma, something that can have a lot to do with whether or not an envelope actually does get opened and your letter has the opportunity to do its job of communicating your message to your recipient.

Try this easy tip: Mark the outside of the envelope with a handwritten message, such as "Look inside for a great offer." The fact that the message is handwritten will differentiate it from the person's address information itself, which is usually typed.

Furthermore, studies have proven that the mere presence of a simple "teaser" message on an envelope will help ensure that the recipient of the envelope (if for no other reason than curiosity) will open the envelope to check out what's inside.

Dear Sharon,

My company will be changing its name. Do you have any hints on how to make sure we don't miss any important items that need to be addressed besides letterhead and business cards? Any ideas on announcements?

Louise, Executive Assistant

Meet with More Success

Dear Louise,

Whenever a company changes its name, there are many details involved, and those details can vary depending on your company, the business you are in and the kinds of customers you do business with. However, here are some general things to keep in mind. In addition to updating your letterhead and business cards as you mentioned, you must also change memo pads that have your company name on them, as well as fax "cover pages" and envelopes. Also, if your company name is part of your e-mail messaging system, change that too. And, any outgoing voice-mail messages that have been recorded with your company name on them must also be updated.

Strategies to help you plan for better business meetings.

Attending meetings is a way of life in almost every business, large and small. Perhaps you conduct a number of different meetings in a typical work week, or maybe you attend very few meetings yourself, yet it's part of your job to help plan and coordinate upcoming meetings for your boss.

The following tips will assist you in making business meetings more successful.

1. **Establish a place to meet and make sure everyone's informed.** It doesn't matter whether the meeting will be held in someone's office, a large conference room, offsite or a call-in—one of the most important things you can do, and certainly one of the most obvious, is to make sure that you pick a meeting location that will be available and will accommodate all attendees. If it's a conference room, chances are it may need to be reserved in advance. Also, once you have the meeting location and date confirmed, be certain that all attendees are notified of the exact date and starting time of the meeting via e-mail or memo.

2. **Prepare an outline.** Everyone in business is extremely busy, so it's important to have a game plan of the meeting's agenda in advance, helping to ensure that time spent at the meeting is spent well. Taking a few moments ahead of time to prepare an outline will provide you and the attendees with a "working script" that can help make the

meeting proceed more smoothly and more efficiently. The outline should include each of the following: an overview of what will be discussed at the meeting, how long the meeting is expected to last, and a time frame for each item on the meeting agenda. Make sure that everyone has the agenda in advance in case someone needs to prepare ahead of time.

3. **Create "take-aways."** Successful business meetings often include printed documents that attendees can refer to during the meeting and then take away from the meeting. These documents drive home the key points discussed at the meeting, helping to reinforce important ideas.

4. **Arrange to have any electronic equipment you may require.** Overhead projectors, multimedia presentation systems and other electronic "bells and whistles" can add immensely to the impact and success of your meeting. Determine well in advance of your meeting what equipment will be needed, reserve it to ensure availability, and also make certain it is in good working order.

5. **Get the gear.** A good business meeting usually involves some sort of equipment that presenters can use to deliver key points. This may include everything from slide or overhead projectors to high-tech multimedia display and sound systems. Determine what will be required and make sure it is all available for the meeting and in perfect working order.

6. **Get graphic.** Virtually all word processing and desktop

publishing applications include clip art illustrations as well as automatic functions that let you create pie charts and bar graphs. Use these in your overheads to add interest and graphic appeal to bulleted points.

7. **Stay short.** Avoid the urge to cram too much on any one overhead. The attention span of most audiences is very limited, so to keep up the pace and excitement of the presentation, it's important to keep moving on to new overheads.

And above all, relax. Business meetings have a way of taking on their own energy, and with the right preparation, they almost always work themselves out to a successful conclusion.

Dear Sharon,

My boss is constantly asking me to create presentation documents for him, and of course, he wants them to look great. Any ways you know of to make it easy for me to do this?

Wendy, Executive Assistant

Dear Wendy,

Making powerful presentations can be the difference between success or failure. There's a smartly
designed line of products called Oxford® Presentation Perfect that could be the ideal solution for you.
With Presentation Perfect, you'll create stunning
presentation portfolios with a customized look in a
matter of moments. The portfolios are specially
designed for use with PowerPoint presentations—
just insert your landscape or portrait pages, and
diagonal corner pockets hold the pages securely.
Plus, the portfolios feature a distinctive linen-like
finish to make a lasting impression!

Re:

More Effective Memos

Five ways to create memos that get noticed and encourage action from co-workers.

Memorandums are those little business notes and reminders
that circulate through your office. At times, you seem to be inundated with one memo after another—and that can mean that
some memos don't even get noticed, let alone acted upon.

Perhaps part of your job entails creating memos that
announce everything from new departmental policies to upcoming special events within your company. The following are five
proven ways to help ensure that the memos you generate achieve

the results you want:

1. **Fewer words, more impact.** In preparing a memo, be careful not to write a book, or even a letter. Keep things short, and the people who receive your memos are more likely to read every word and absorb what you're saying.

2. **Bullet your thoughts.** Readership studies about office memos (yes, there are such studies) show that utilizing bulleted copy points to stress key ideas, instead of using paragraphs, can make a memo more inviting to the reader and enhance the overall impact of the memo.

3. **Solicit feedback.** Another smart way to add impact to your memos is to engage the reader personally by asking them to get back to you. For example, perhaps the memo is about the implementation of a new system for filing invoices. In the memo, request that your readers take action by submitting back to you their own ideas for the new system.

4. **Become multimedia savvy.** Not all memos are written on paper. Many are also sent electronically via e-mail. If you really want to be sure that your memos reach everyone, combine the two and circulate memos to co-workers both in the old-fashioned paper way and also through cyberspace.

5. **"CC" the people in charge.** When preparing your list of who will receive your memos, always remember to put the people you report to (and possibly the people they report to) in the loop. Including the names of top man-

agement in the "cc" section of your memo not only keeps everyone informed, it also brings importance and urgency to the memo itself.

Conventional Wisdom

Got a trade show coming up?
Learn smart tips for preparing successfully.

If you're an old pro at getting ready to participate in a trade show, then you've been through it all before. However, perhaps you've been asked for the first time to coordinate your company's trip to a show. After doing many trade shows, I have learned that you need to be prepared for anything and always bring your creative hat with you. There will be times when you will have to punt. I have had a range of unforeseen experiences from a booth missing parts to product not showing up. Whether the exhibit is a simple table-top event, or a full-blown convention, here are a few tips I learned to help make your job easier:

1. **Plan early.** This sounds logical enough, but you'd be surprised how many trade-show planners wait until the very last moment to address what's needed to participate in the show. Even with early planning, you can always expect the unexpected. So be prepared to get creative. More times than I would like to remember, what I thought I could count on I couldn't. Some things are out of your

control especially if the show is on a weekend.

2. **Create lists.** Getting ready for a trade show involves a myriad of tasks. These may include booking rooms for attendees, rounding up product samples for display on the show floor, making sure that enough support literature is shipped to the show, arranging for cocktail parties during the event, and many, many other things. At the beginning of your planning efforts, spend some time typing it all up on a "to-do" list, then check off each item as you accomplish it.

3. **Get to know the territory.** Sometime during the early planning stages of your trade show, phone ahead to the convention venue and ask that they send you a layout of the show floor indicating exactly where your booth will be positioned. This will assist your fellow associates who will "work the booth" in getting a feel for their surroundings ahead of time.

4. **Draw up a game plan for all the players.** Veteran trade-show planners are often amazed how helpless some executives can seem when they're no longer on "familiar turf." Weeks before the show, prepare a complete agenda of all the activities that will take place. Include such items as departure and arrival times, where everyone will stay, what meetings they will need to attend, even suggestions for leisure activities. This will help put everyone's mind at ease and give them confidence that you've covered all the bases. Most important, have a pre-conference meeting

with everyone involved and a follow-up after the show to discuss what worked and what didn't.

5. **Follow up, and follow up some more.** Making arrangements for travel, exhibit floor space, accommodations and other aspects of trade-show planning are all part of the process of ensuring a successful show. And so is checking back to make certain each of these things is being taken care of. Be sure to make follow-up phone calls with travel agents and other outside people—as well as inside personnel—to receive periodic status reports. Following up before the show can be the difference between success and disaster.

6. **Have contingency plans in place.** As careful as you are in planning a trade show, some things may go wrong. And although you cannot predict the future and don't want to dwell on negatives, try to anticipate things that could possibly go awry, so you'll be ready if they do.

Building a Better Bash

How to plan a successful office party or gathering at home.

So, the "Big Cheese" is retiring or you need to plan a special occasion party and you've been put in charge. Lucky you. Not to worry, here are a few straightforward yet proven tips for making sure the occasion is an affair to remember.

1. **Prepare ahead.** It seems obvious, but lack of preparation gets a lot of people in trouble as the date of the party fast approaches. Granted, you won't always have months (or even weeks) to get your act together, but you must still make sure that several "musts" are arranged ahead of time, including:

   ✓ Reserving the venue. Whether it's a conference room, a catering hall or someone's home, be certain it's available;

   ✓ ordering enough food and/or drinks; and

   ✓ sending out the invitations in time for people to plan on being there.

2. **Have an agenda.** The best parties don't just run their own course to a successful conclusion. You need a clear idea ahead of time as to what will occur, how it will occur and when. For example, if the bash is being held at a restaurant, will everyone gather at the bar, then sit down for dinner? Will there be dancing? Will there be speeches by company execs? Run through all the scenarios in your mind so you are well prepared to keep the evening moving smoothly and seamlessly.

3. **Do something unique.** Sure, the party could be like every other office gathering or social get-together you've ever attended. But why? Consider a theme to your party. For instance, if you're celebrating the success of the Western Sales Division, why not have party attendees dress in

authentic Western gear? Other ideas that work well are situations that get people involved. If the party is designed to observe the holidays, how about having a "grab bag" where partygoers can secretly pick names ahead of time then place them in the bag for exchanging gifts at the party?

4. **And finally, keep your wits about you.** Chances are, even with the best planning, your party will have glitches as it progresses. Whatever you do, don't panic! Stay focused on solving the problem at hand, whether it's sending out for more ice or reporting to the electric company that the lights just went out in the middle of your dinner. Address the situation calmly, and you'll be surprised how everything will work itself out in the end.

These are some very important issues that can be the difference between disaster and success.

CHAPTER 9

REDUCING STRESS

Really Keeping Your ACT Together

The business world, and life in general, seems to move at a lightning pace. Companies are downsizing and asking more of the employees. Working parents are pulled in all directions and life is just more hectic. The result can be heightened pressure and that can cause stress. As we all know, stress has the potential to contribute to health problems. However, stress can be managed and in many cases reduced. This chapter has some simple suggestions you may want to try for yourself.

Stressed Out?

Simple ideas for lowering your stress levels in today's hectic offices, or how to keep your cool when the pressure gets hot.

Today's office environment—fueled by high-speed Internet connections, blazing fast computers and ever-present deadlines—can be a very stressful place to work. And if you're a working parent, you may wonder how you can possibly do it all.

Thankfully, there are proven ways to relieve the pressure that can build as your day proceeds. The following are some great techniques to help you relax and keep your cool in the office and at home:

1. **Deep breathing.** Inhale as much as you possibly can, filling your chest completely. Then exhale slowly, emptying all the air you just breathed in. Repeat several times.

2. **Positive imagery.** Close your eyes and visualize an atmosphere that you perceive to be relaxing, such as a country meadow or a quiet trail in the woods. Concentrate on the image for several seconds; you'll be surprised how this can calm you down.

3. **Let your body go limp.** While seated in your office chair, imagine that you are a rag doll. Concentrate on letting your arms and legs become completely limp, as if they have no power to support themselves.

4. **Change your outlook.** If possible, go to a window (or

step outside) and focus on something far off in the distance. Stare at the object for at least twenty seconds, thinking about nothing but that object.

5. **Redirect your thoughts for a moment.** When things get particularly stressful on the job, you sometimes need to take your mind completely away from the office. A good way to do this is by phoning a friend or relative and talking about anything but work. If making a call is not possible, look at a photograph of a friend and recount in your mind the fun times you've had together, or, look at photos of a favorite vacation place and momentarily relive the good time you had there.

Try each of the above relaxation techniques to see which ones work best for you in addressing daily pressures. Below are easy techniques for preventing and alleviating at least some of the stress associated with working in today's fast-paced offices:

1. **Know your limits.** If taking on two extra projects last week pushed you to the extreme, be aware that taking on three this week could put you over the edge. In other words, you don't always have to go the extra mile every time your boss asks you to. Most supervisors would rather see quality work, even if it means sacrificing quantity.

2. **Take your time.** If you have vacation coming to you, use it. You've earned it, and more importantly, your body and your mind need it to rejuvenate.

3. **Don't be afraid to delegate.** Just because the boss asked you personally to do something doesn't mean you can't ask for help. If the job genuinely requires assistance from a co-worker, request it. The boss will understand.

4. **Stay organized, stay on schedule.** When you begin a new project, establish a schedule at the beginning by making a list of all you need to do. Then stick to the plan. This is far less stressful than taking a haphazard "seat of your pants" approach.

5. **Give yourself a break.** If you're working on something particularly tedious, take a few moments every half hour or so to relax and focus your mind on something else. Perhaps take a short stroll in the hallway, or get some coffee. These "mini breaks" can work wonders in reducing your stress levels.

Worry Less, Do More

Three strategies to help you stop derailing productivity by obsessing about things at work.

We all worry to some extent; after all, it's just human nature. However, too much worry—oftentimes unnecessarily—can get in the way of completing office projects because an excessive amount of our thought processes and our energy are spent concentrating on the source of the worry.

What begins as a small worry may sometimes lead to an obsession that in some cases can entirely thwart productivity. Here are three simple-to-implement strategies that may help you reduce office worries and be able to get more done:

1. **Be your own judge.** At times, people who work in offices become overly worried that they're not living up to the expectations of others. Most commonly, it's the boss who is perceived as the person who is putting undue pressure on the situation. Sure, the boss makes the rules and sets the goals, but it's you that makes it happen. And yes, you want to sometimes "go the extra mile" to prove how good you are at your job, but try not to get caught in a trap of constantly attempting to over-impress the boss. Instead, be confident in your ability to determine for yourself that you are indeed doing a good job.

2. **Be there for the moment.** It can be easy to let your mind wander ahead, obsessing about a coming deadline or spending too much of your thought process thinking about what's in store for the future. Problem is, when you worry too much about things to come, you lose focus on immediate tasks. Make a conscious effort to direct most if not all of your attention to what you're doing now—you may find that you worry less while also allowing yourself to complete a current task more productively.

3. **If you must, designate some "worry time."** Obviously, it's nearly impossible for most people to eliminate worry from their lives altogether. One solution might be to schedule an actual "worry session," perhaps fifteen minutes each week.

By specifically designating a time to concentrate on what's worrying you, you'll be less likely to spend productive time doing so. Plus, you may often find that your worries are really not worth a full fifteen minutes, and that can give you a boost of positive energy!

Although on a different note, the following letters are two other examples of how your stress level can be elevated.

Dear Sharon,

This is more a pet peeve and a suggestion than a question. Nothing irks me more than to call someone and, after introducing myself and stating my business, to be transferred to someone else. [Then], I am again transferred to someone else. This could go on through several folks. I know that this gripes me to no end, so what I do and I wish that so many others would do is when transferring a call to "Miss X," I tell Miss X who is on the other end and what their business is. [That way] when Miss X takes over the call, she begins by saying "Hello Mr. B, I'm told that you are calling to inquire about _____ (whatever)." This should make Mr. B very happy that he doesn't have to repeat his name or [the reason for his call] once again, after having done it three or four times already. Thanks for letting me sound off.

Denise, Administrative Assistant

Dear Denise,

Thanks for the input, and remember, giving people a forum for sounding off about things relating to the office is one of the reasons we're here. As you know, I've already e-mailed you back stating that I agree with you, getting the runaround on the phone is no way to spend your workday—particularly when you're busy and staring at a tough deadline. I am reprinting your suggestion in this newsletter so that the rest of our I Hate Filing Club members can read about your excellent suggestion for remedying a problem that unfortunately is all too common in today's business world!

Dear Sharon,

How [do I] handle a case where a co-worker is being checked on and I am being asked if the person is in the office or have I seen her today or what time did she leave because she has chosen to take classes during her work time. I don't like the space I am in. Help.

Brenda, Secretary

Dear Brenda,

Sounds like you are indeed in a tough spot. First of all, approach your co-worker directly and tell her you are not comfortable covering for her as it could jeopardize your own job. And when asked questions by your superiors, the best policy is always to tell the truth, though I'm guessing that you would rather not be put in the position of answering for the whereabouts of someone you work with. If your supervisors persist, my advice is to go ahead and tell them what you know. In the final analysis, your co-worker, not you, must be made responsible for the way she conducts herself at work.

Keep the Office Fires Burning

How to avoid burnout at work

Did you know that according to worldwide industry studies, Americans put in longer hours than workers of any other industrialized nation?

The average American spends 1,966 hours at work annually, compared with 1,890 in Japan; 1,731 in Britain; 1,717 in Italy; 1,656 in France; and 1,574 in Germany.

As a result, most American workers—particularly those who toil in hectic offices—are prone to a growing phenomenon: burnout.

Here are some tips to help avoid the possibility of becoming a basket case because of too much work.

1. **Scale back.** Sure, it's tough to cut down on your workload when the boss is constantly dumping projects on you. But it doesn't hurt to say no once in a while if you're reaching your breaking point. The boss may not realize you have more than you can handle, and he or she will probably appreciate your honesty.

2. **Give yourself a break.** There's no need to put constant pressure on yourself to be a "hero." Try not to overcommit your time and your resources to unrealistic deadlines and assignments.

3. **Set limits.** At the beginning of each week, create a list of what you need to accomplish that week. Concentrate on finishing what is on the list before you begin new projects.

4. **Steer away from things that can drive you nuts.** If there's a controversy at work, do everything you can not to get involved. By getting in the middle of a mess, you'll only raise your own blood pressure.

5. **Take what's coming to you.** You've earned your vacation time and if you don't take it because "things are too crazy at work," you're cheating yourself and risking the possibility of becoming overstressed. As the old adage goes, the work will be there when you get back.

Most importantly, take time for family. Children grow up so quickly, you don't want to regret those missed times. Watching your kid's Little League or soccer game or a dance recital can be a great energizer. Being a single mom, it wasn't always easy to take that time from work, but it was the one rule I made with any job I had. In fact I set that ground rule from day one. Looking back, it was the best thing I did.

CHAPTER 10

SELF-IMPROVEMENT STRATEGIES

Ways to Make Goals a Reality

Almost all of us have goals, and we constantly strive to achieve them. Perhaps your goal is to become better at your job, to create more opportunities to increase your salary, and also to receive more personal and professional satisfaction from the work you do. Maybe it's time to start that business you've always dreamed about. Here are several insights that could help you improve the way you do things.

But Seriously, Folks

Tips for making sure you and your ideas are taken seriously, whether you are a seasoned employee or new.

You know the type: the person in your office who's always goofing around, telling lots of jokes, making everyone laugh. Sure, they're popular and great to have around. But they never seem to get any significant promotions, any real recognition or any big raises. There's a reason—no one takes them or what they say seriously.

Of course, we're not suggesting that you have to be a "stick in the mud" and be all business all the time. There certainly are appropriate times to let your hair down and have fun at work. However, if you really want to get ahead in today's competitive business world, it's important that you follow a few basic rules, including:

1. **Speaking with conviction.** When you believe in your ideas, and that belief is evident in the tone of your voice, the people around you (including your superiors) are likely to share your enthusiasm and view your ideas as good ones.

2. **Dressing appropriately.** If you dress like a teenager, chances are you might be perceived as one and not seen as a person who can handle large amounts of responsibility. You should dress for the position you want, not the position you have.

3. **Remain positive.** Complainers are almost always stymied in their quest to gain recognition and advancement at work. When you think and act negatively, you are not viewed as a "team player," and that can really work against you.

4. **Offering specific solutions.** When a problem arises, instead of focusing on the hardship it may cause you and your co-workers, seek logical solutions that address the problem right away. This will position you as a self-starter and a person who can take charge of a situation.

5. **Being on time in the morning.** Better yet, be early. This should probably go without saying, however, if you show up late for work on a steady basis you are communicating to your superiors that you are not really committed to your job—a sure way to stall any potential promotions.

Below are two important tips for new employees.

✓ **Learn the territory.** If you are a new employee, an important step in transitioning well to a new job is to get to know where everything is. Most likely, your new supervisor will offer to take you on a tour of your new department, your new building and/or facility. Take special note of the location of important destinations, such as the bathrooms, the lunchroom, the copy machine and the mail room.

✓ **Extend a hand.** Your first few days at a new job will

include meeting new people. Be sure to make your new co-workers feel that you're very glad to make their acquaintance by quickly offering a handshake, smiling and making solid eye contact. These types of body-language approaches will communicate an openness and friendliness about you, urging co-workers to help you adjust to your new position.

Try adhering to the above suggestions, and think of them as rules to remember for moving up the corporate ladder. You might be surprised how a few simple, yet noticeable, changes in your approach to your job or business can get you on the fast track and put a larger paycheck in your pocket.

Damage Control

Everybody makes mistakes at work; Here's how to prevent them from ruining your day.

It happens to everyone, in all kinds of companies and in just about every situation you can think of—we're talking about boo boos, blunders, foul-ups. Any way you refer to it, mistakes are a fact of life.

For instance, perhaps you've missed a vital deadline and your boss is giving you plenty of heat for it. Or, maybe you lost an important document that was needed for an upcoming presentation.

The key thing to remember is, as the old axiom goes, "to err is human." I remember my first job in the big city. I was responsible for writing airline tickets in the corporate travel department. It's been more than twenty-five years but I remember clearly the day I sent the president of the company to the wrong airport!

Mistakes do indeed happen, and, yes, some mistakes are bigger than others. However, instead of letting the mishap destroy your workday and become a hindrance to your future job performance, you need to deal with the mistake right away and learn from it.

Here are a few tips for handling mistakes on the job:

1. **Take responsibility.** One of the first things that many people do when a work-related blunder occurs is to place the blame on someone else. This only worsens the situation. Stand up, take the blame and demonstrate to your boss that you're ready and capable of rectifying the situation.

2. **Look for solutions, not excuses.** Much like trying to place the blame on someone else, people in busy offices will often waste time and energy explaining why the mistake might have happened—rather than putting their energy into fixing the problem. Being proactive and results oriented can actually work in your favor in the eyes of your boss, showing that you can deal with adversity and be a self-starter who is committed to finding solutions.

3. **Move on.** Dwelling on a mistake will only make things worse and could cause you to lose concentration, which could lead to other mistakes. Put the mishap behind you,

instead of allowing it to fester and become even bigger than it has to be.

4. **Take preventive measures.** Obviously, when you make a mistake at work, you don't want it to happen again. Consider all the factors that led to the blunder, then take steps to make certain the same thing does not happen again.

Dear Sharon,

I had a really bad office blunder the other day and I just wanted to warn some other people about the potential for disaster. My boss asked me to have some award certificates framed and while getting ready to take them to the framing place, I left the certificates on my desk, and then I spilled an entire cup of coffee on them. They were ruined and I had to explain why to my boss. I guess it's all because my desk is so messy to begin with, and I've heard you mention how important it is to keep your desk clean of clutter. From now on I will.

Lisa, Administrative Supervisor

Dear Lisa,

Sorry to hear about your unfortunate coffee spill. I'm certain that the certificates were valuable and I'm sure it was very difficult to go to your boss and tell how they got ruined. Yes, keeping your desk clutter-free might have avoided the accident, and here's another way: a high quality line of water-resistant filing products called Pendaflex® Watershed® File Folders. Watershed folders are specially made to protect important documents from common desk spills, rain and other moisture damage. Another product solution is using poly file folders; although more expensive, they will protect your papers from any spills.

Take This Job and Love It

Four tips that can help you enjoy life in the office more.

Perhaps there are days that you force yourself out of bed, trudge into work, and do not look forward to the struggles of another day in the office. You're not alone. Studies indicate that more than half of American workers claim to dislike their jobs.

Yet, just about all of us realize that we have to work. And, moving from job to job in hopes of finding the perfect one is not always an option.

Well, why not look at things another way? Why not try some strategies that could actually help you love, or at least enjoy, your work? Here are four suggestions:

1. **Volunteer for high-visibility projects.** Maybe the boss, or the boss's boss, has a huge meeting coming up and she or he needs some dazzling handouts that you could design on your computer. By "putting yourself out there" and volunteering for projects that everyone is likely to see and appreciate, you'll stimulate your creative juices, which can give you more fulfillment—and yes, enjoyment—from your work.

2. **Expand your horizons.** How about taking a course at your local college or university? Maybe you're an expert in Word for Windows, but you want to learn more about PowerPoint. Expanding your horizons by taking an online course could give you a whole new outlook on your job!

3. **Invite new challenges.** Want that promotion? Go for it. Your company may have certain committees in place, for instance, a "new business development" committee. Join in, make yourself heard, challenge yourself to come up with new ideas. The end result could be very rewarding.

4. **Network.** You might be surprised how "rubbing elbows" with other professionals can change the way you perceive

your job. Chances are, they are faced with challenges, both actual and motivational, just like you. Exchanging thoughts about how to gain more enjoyment from your work could be just the solution you're looking for.

Turn Lemons into Lemonade

Five ways to make the best of bad situations at work.

Certainly, there are any number of things that can be a challenge to deal with when you work in an office. Although you've probably experienced many more negatives in the office than those listed here, we've addressed what are perhaps the most common dilemmas—and we offer straightforward suggestions to help you make the best of them. We spoke about this in a previous chapter but it bears repeating.

1. **A difficult boss.** This is probably the number one and most persistent problem the average office worker is faced with. The best way to address this situation is through communication. Rather than sitting back and continually steaming over a boss who is overbearing and demanding beyond belief, request a meeting where you can get a clearer picture of exactly what is expected of you. You may be surprised to learn that just by talking things out, your boss will respect you more and may even give you added latitude in performing your job. Remember the tip I gave previously: Try

finding one thing you like about this person; you'd be surprised to see what a difference it makes.

2. **Annoying co-workers.** You work with the same people every day, and naturally, you want to get along with everyone. However, there might be one person you simply cannot stand. Avoid confronting this person because that will only inflame the situation. As tough as it might seem, your best strategy is to not let this person throw your game off. In other words, try to ignore the annoying person(s) as much as possible.

3. **Stress.** Pressure and continual time constraints affect everyone differently, but one of the best things to do is take a periodic time-out. A simple walk in the hall, a trip to the coffee station, a phone call to a loved one—these can all work wonders in calming you down.

4. **Constant interruptions.** Try and stop them in their tracks by eliminating them. For instance, unless your job specifically requires you to answer the phone, let your voice mail take the call during times when you're particularly busy. Also during busy times, try to limit (or at least shorten) visits from co-workers who stop by to chat and thereby disrupt your workflow.

5. **Huge workload.** Obviously, you don't want to do anything to jeopardize your job, such as refusing to work on a project. At the same time, you don't want to jeopardize your health. It's possible that your boss may not be aware that you're overloaded. You don't always have to be the one who takes

on every project all by yourself. Once in a while, request assistance.

Me, Myself and I

Five tips to help you look out for number one in a competitive office.

Everyone wants to succeed in their business life. And most of us care a great deal about our co-workers. However, you can't ignore the fact that not everyone can get the big promotion they really want, which means that the majority of the time you are actually competing against your co-workers to get recognized and "climb the corporate ladder" at your company.

While we're not suggesting in any way that you become selfish or cutthroat in your quest to move ahead, you might want to consider the following tips to help ensure that you "protect your turf" in today's highly competitive office environment:

1. **Document your achievements.** When review time comes around and you're in position for a promotion or raise, it's a good idea to have something in writing that shows what you accomplished. As the year progresses, jot down your successes in order to create a written record of what you've achieved.

2. **Remain neutral.** Invariably, controversies arise in an office setting. Perhaps two people don't get along, or

someone feels that the boss is out to get them. Avoid taking sides in such disputes because this could alienate people while also stalling your potential for career advancement.

3. **Get out there.** Try to volunteer for certain high-visibility projects when they are available. For instance, maybe you could assist the boss on a big year-end presentation he or she is preparing for the top brass. However, don't offer to take on just any project; avoid projects that you may not be able to handle because this could overextend your abilities and make you appear in a negative light.

4. **Dance to your own beat.** Make efforts to think on your own, rather than always going along with the crowd in your office. In other words, create an image for yourself as a leader, not a follower, thus enhancing promotion opportunities.

5. **Align yourself properly.** Naturally, you would like everyone in your company to be your friend, but having friends in high places is one of the surest ways to look out for your future. Don't be afraid to form friendships with people in your company who are in positions of power—they could become very valuable.

Your Moment in the Sun

How to take credit for a job well done (without sounding boastful).

You did it, that enormous customer report the boss assigned to you has been completed—with overwhelming success! Now, co-workers in your office are patting you on the back and they're also wanting to know how in the heck you were able to achieve what you did.

Sure, you're anxious (like any other human being) to bask in the spotlight of your achievement, but you don't want anyone to think you're bragging. Here are some suggestions for enjoying the accolades without the attitude:

1. **Eat just a little humble pie.** Everyone has already noticed your success. There's really no need to spout off about the details. As the old cliché goes, "Actions speak louder than words" and your actions have told the story more effectively than your words ever could.

2. **Share the wealth.** Yes, enjoy the adulation, but if someone else in your office has assisted you in your achievement do not hesitate to also give them credit. This will demonstrate that you are a team player—a highly promote-able trait!

3. **Focus on the big picture.** Another way to still enjoy

accolades for a job well done but not sound boastful is to mention how your success may benefit the company. For instance, perhaps you've developed a new and more productive system for filing customer sales receipts. And that system will save hours each week in administrative time (as well as money). In accepting congratulations for your idea, try and also briefly point out that you feel "especially satisfied that what I've done can make a real difference to the company's bottom line."

4. **Point to the future.** Still another approach to taking credit for a work success without sounding boastful is to be proactive, demonstrating that although you're proud of what you've done you don't intend to dwell on it, instead you are anxious to create new successes.

Resolution Revolution

When each new year approaches, four simple changes in your work habits can change your whole outlook.

It seems that every year, everyone enters January with the best of intentions. Most of the time, New Year's resolutions involve strategies for improving the ways we go about our lives. And while each person has their own unique ideas about what works best for them in the office, there are certain things you can do that will change (and could enhance) the way you approach your daily life and work routines. Since January is National Get Organized Month, I thought this would be a good approach to getting the new year off to a good start.

1. **Avoid procrastination.** Putting things off only adds to the stress of hectic office life because it gives you more time to worry about such things as impending deadlines. Also, waiting until the last moment to complete a project forces you to rush, creating opportunities for mistakes.

2. **Try a little kindness.** Stomping around the office mad at the world is no way to work effectively. You'll be surprised how much more receptive your co-workers will be to you, how eager they will be to help you, and how much more satisfaction you can take away from your job by simply being nice to everyone you work with all the time.

3. **Be prompt.** As mentioned before, showing up tardy in the morning or coming back late from lunch, or handing in departmental assignments beyond their deadline will obviously not be perceived favorably by your boss. In addition to the negative image it can create for you, not being on time in your professional life can really make your blood pressure rise because you'll find yourself constantly looking at the clock and trying to move at four hundred miles an hour to catch up. Yes, always being on time in your work life can be difficult with such personal demands as children and various home activities, but it's something that can truly change you for the better.

4. **Take vacations.** Perhaps you go year to year and don't always use all your vacation time. The question is, why? You've earned the time, you deserve it, and above all, you need it to regroup mentally and recharge physically.

Forget You Not

Four easy tips for remembering things in the office.

Deadlines, meetings, appointments, the latest rush request from your boss . . . it probably seems that you have a million things on your mind. With so much going on in the office, and thoughts of kids, friends and other outside considerations also stirring in your head during your workday, it can be hard to remember every little detail.

Here are four techniques that may help (tying a string around your finger is not one of them):

1. **How to remember "to do" tasks:** Jot down the steps you need to complete on a list. This seems very obvious, but it amazes us how many office workers we talk to who do not make a list of the things they need to accomplish during their workday. They instead tend to "wing it" through the day, creating opportunities for certain tasks to get overlooked and important project priorities to be temporarily forgotten.

2. **How to remember deadlines:** Post self-stick reminder

notes on your computer monitor, your desk or a shelf near where you work. These will provide a constant and visible reminder of when a particular project is due, making it easier for you to stay on schedule.

3. **How to remember appointments:** Get yourself a good appointment book. Once again, as with lists, many people we ask tell us that although they are always going to meetings or planning some sort of appointment for a future date, they don't always jot down the date and time of the meeting in an appointment book. Many times, they simply try to remember the occasion in their heads, which of course can lead to a missed appointment. Or, they scribble the information on a scrap of paper, only to lose the paper and subsequently forget about the appointment.

4. **How to remember names:** Just about anyone who works in an office is always meeting new people . . . customers, new employees, etc. It can be difficult to remember the name of each person. Try this technique: Upon being introduced, repeat the name of the person you are being introduced to. In fact you should try repeating it three times. For instance: Hi Sharon, I am pleased to meet you; Sharon, let me ask you a question; Thanks, Sharon, that was a great answer. Get the idea? This will help embed the name in your mind.

Dear Sharon,

I am having difficulty remembering how to do certain paperwork that I have done before. I am not comfortable about [having] someone else [perform these paperwork tasks] because I feel intimidated. Do you have a suggestion for a way of keeping up with previous paperwork on the same type of task so I don't have to rely on my failing memory?

Ann, Secretary

Dear Ann,

First of all, why feel intimidated? Be confident in your abilities; paperwork is part of office life and it's nothing to worry about. Besides, as a member of the I Hate Filing Club, you have one of the world's most informed paperwork-management resources at your disposal, as you can probably see from the many tips and insights we offer about managing paperwork each month in this newsletter. As for remembering paperwork tasks and keeping up with previous work, my suggestion is to make a list of those tasks. Write it all down, then as you finish each task, cross it off the list. This will keep you up to date and also give you a sense of accomplishment as tasks are completed and crossed off!

Authoritative Source

Four strategies for being perceived as "the person to ask" in the office.

If you've worked in an office for any length of time, you've probably noticed that there always seems to be someone in the office who supervisors and co-workers turn to in order to get answers—whether it's the status of a certain project, background about a customer or information about "such and such" file.

These are all topics that you have the answers to, and perhaps you want to be the "go-to" person because you realize that demonstrating your expertise is a great way to position yourself for promotions, more office responsibility and bigger raises.

So, how exactly do you generate the perception that you are the "person to ask" in your office? Because you already have the knowledge, much of that perception has to do with how you answer the questions themselves. In other words, what you say is important, but how you say it can be just as vital.

Here are four strategies:

1. **Keep your hands to yourself.** Business communication experts advise that making flailing gestures with your arms while speaking can detract from what you're saying and take some credibility from your words. Also, do not play with your hair while speaking.

2. **Say it with conviction.** The tone of your voice itself can

have a lot to do with the perception of you as an authority on certain topics. Speak clearly and make sure to enunciate each word. Try also to avoid "ums" and "uhs" as you speak.

3. **Tell no tales.** Even white lies can come back to haunt you, and, obviously, if you're caught in one it will undermine your credibility. Even though you want to be an authority on many things in your office, not everyone can be expected to know absolutely everything.

4. **Leave the questions to the asker.** When someone asks for your advice, knowledge or opinion, state your answer as just that, an answer. Avoid a habit that many people have, raising their voice at the end of their response so that it sounds as though they're answering a question with another question. This can indicate you're unsure of your answer.

Going for the Juggler

Today's companies want people who can multitask, so give these approaches a try.

One of the most important things you can do to make yourself more valuable to either your current employer or a potential one is to demonstrate your ability to juggle many office projects and responsibilities—simultaneously.

Consider the following ideas for making yourself more proficient at the vital art of multitasking:

1. **Allocate specific times for specific tasks.** Instead of plowing forward with no rhyme or reason time-wise, make a schedule for yourself at the beginning of each day. For example, designate 9 A.M.–10 A.M. for correspondence such as returning phone calls or writing memos; 10 A.M.–11 A.M. for filing; and so on. You'll find that by concentrating only on one task during a given period of time, you'll be more proficient at each task throughout your day.

2. **Prioritize.** Obviously, some projects you work on will have tighter deadlines than others. But you'd be surprised how many people ignore such a simple fact. To be most productive overall, you need to manage deadlines in the best way possible by attacking your projects in the order they are due. Remember multitasking does not mean working on more than one project at the exact same time.

3. **Solicit help when needed.** No one can truly expect you to be able to do the work of five people. When an especially involved project comes along, do not be afraid to ask your boss if it's possible to form a small team so that the project can be completed quickly and accurately.

4. **Write it down.** In the first chapter and throughout this book, we've talked about the importance of making lists and writing down goals. Without them, things can slip through the cracks, particularly when you're multitasking a large number of responsibilities. Also, as tasks are completed, remember to cross them off your list, giving you an instant overview of what's been done and what still needs to be done.

This would be a great time to take a look at the list you made in the first chapter. How did you do with your goals? Were you able to establish goals for yourself? Some of those goals could be a promotion, a raise, enrolling in school, getting a higher grade, spending more time with your family. Whatever your personal goals are, did you write down short-term goals that will help you achieve your long-term goal? By now you should be able to see what obstacles are in your way to achieving what you need and want from life.

5. **Take a breather.** Many fast-track multitaskers frequently get caught in the trap of never stopping to catch their breath, and trying to do too much all the time. To be the best you can be at multitasking, it's important to recharge on a regular basis by treating yourself to a coffee break. Also, make sure not to make a habit of skipping lunch.

Dear Sharon,

My desk is such a mess!!! I never seem to finish a project. The interruptions are constant. Everyone has something that is more important than the last one. If a strong wind blew through here I'd be in big trouble. Can you help me get more organized???

Susan, Personal Secretary

Dear Susan,

As anyone who has read this newsletter before knows, my message about a messy desk never varies: Clean it up immediately by putting papers into the file, removing excess knickknacks and other items that can take up valuable work space, and generally making the centerpiece of your workday more "workable." You would be amazed how many people tell me that each day in the office seems easier and projects get finished faster with a clutter-free desk, simply because they don't have to waste time and get frustrated plowing through piles of papers every time they need to locate something. And as for the interruptions from people who have continually "more important" projects for you to work on, you must prioritize. Believe it or not, nobody really expects you to be superhuman and able to complete a hundred projects all at the same time. When someone asks you to do something, take a moment, catch your breath and consider the time frame in which the task is needed. Perhaps even create a list for referencing all the things you need to do in a given day—and as each task is completed cross it off the list. This keeps you better organized and also helps to ensure that certain tasks don't get overlooked.

Rejecting the Notion

When ideas are rejected at work, the impulse is to take it personally. Here's how not to.

It can be painful at times, that empty feeling in the pit of your stomach that comes with knocking yourself out to come up with what you think is "the next big idea" for your company or department—only to have your idea shot down.

The natural reaction for many people is instant disappointment, maybe even anger, and the feeling that the rejection of an idea could go further than the idea itself and could also be a personal criticism. As you might guess, that kind of reaction can be counterproductive, possibly causing you to withdraw and to allow negative thoughts to dominate your work approach.

Fact is, ideas are rejected all the time in offices large and small. Many of those ideas are indeed terrific ones, but nevertheless, they are still turned down. The best tactic to take if that happens? Do not allow yourself to consider the rejection of your idea as a personal attack. In the long run, you'll be better for it.

The following are some insights about how not to take rejection at work personally:

1. **Distance yourself for a moment.** Resist the urge to become emotionally upset over the rejection of your idea. Instead, take a deep breath, collect your thoughts and step back until you clear your head. Chances are by taking a

short "time-out," your outlook about the situation will improve.

2. **Remember that business is business.** Many times, ideas are rejected simply because they don't match the business plans of the company you work for or the department you work in. If your idea is rejected, remind yourself that although you could have the most creative and most unique proposal in the world, if it's determined that your approach is not aligned with the objectives at hand, the idea will probably not move forward.

3. **Accept the challenge.** You know in your heart that the original idea was great, but what the heck, it didn't fly. So challenge yourself to come up with a new idea; you may surprise even yourself at your ability to do so, and at the same time, you'll demonstrate your versatility to your boss.

CHAPTER 11

ADVANCING YOUR CAREER

Staying Ahead of the Curve

Moving ahead in business is no easy task. It takes hard work, dedication, experience and knowledge. In this chapter, we'll provide some tips, techniques and suggestions that might just provide the knowledge you need to assist in furthering your career. You should always be open; you never know where your next opportunity will come from. The first part of this chapter will help you with getting the raise and promotion you deserve. The second half will help you when it's time to move on.

Upward Mobility

Strategies for getting the promotion you really want.

You work hard. You do and say all the right things and project a positive attitude. And you keep getting good job reviews. But somehow, you're constantly being passed over for a promotion.

Maybe it's time to really go for it, to take a proactive approach so you can get the promotion and the pay raise you know you've earned.

Here are some tips for increasing your opportunities to move up in the competitive corporate world:

1. **Prove your worth.** Sometimes, it's simply not enough to do a great job and hope everyone notices. Try documenting some of the things you do. For instance, if you come up with a creative new way to route paperwork throughout your office—and your idea saves time and money for the company—calculate exactly how much time and money you think it amounts to and let your boss know the savings are due to your efforts.

2. **Do something more.** Perhaps your job only requires you to answer phones. But maybe the phones aren't ringing all the time, so use your spare moments to do something else, such as updating the customer contact list for your boss. This will demonstrate your willingness and ability to do more than what your current job requires.

3. **Make yourself indispensable.** Of course, this is easier said than done. But consider this example: If your job entails typing up presentations for corporate executives, take the job a step further and actually show the bosses that you can also design graphically dynamic overheads using your desktop software. How much more valuable do you think this would make you?

4. **Lobby your case.** Don't be afraid to sit down with your boss and discuss your ambitions and communicate your qualifications for a promotion. Sometimes, bosses simply don't realize that one of their associates would make a great candidate for a higher level job.

5. **Take credit where credit is due.** Many times, office workers shy away from the limelight when accolades are given for the successful completion of a project. This can be due to an introverted nature, or perhaps the fear that accepting congratulations for doing a great job may put added pressure on future projects. Do not be afraid to accept credit when it is given to you. Of course, being humble is a characteristic that everyone in your office will appreciate, yet being confident about what you have accomplished indicates that more of the same will come. And that's a great way of making the bosses take notice of your abilities to handle a job promotion.

6. **Volunteer for high-profile projects.** Perhaps a large presentation is planned for the biggest customer your department or company deals with. Volunteer to become

involved in the development of the presentation, lending your best skills—whether it's creating meeting handouts or compiling the presentation documents in a fast and neat way. The point is, by being part of highly visible projects you will in turn increase your own visibility.

7. **Show excitement.** You've heard the phrase before: Excitement can be contagious. When a huge (and visible) project arises, demonstrate that you are genuinely passionate about making the project the very best it can be. Co-workers and management personnel alike are certain to notice your positive attitude and perceive you as an important contributor to the eventual success of the project.

Dear Sharon:

I am frustrated with my job although I like it. I am frustrated because I do the same thing every day. I am frustrated that I have not moved up for the last nineteen years. I have interviewed for higher level positions but not been offered them. I have applied for reclassification but not received a high level position. Currently my second reclassification request is somewhere on the director's desk. I am feeling stuck and have let my B.S. degree somewhat go to waste. Can you help me with my effort to achieve a higher level position? Thanks.

Barbara, Secretary

Dear Barbara,

Feeling frustrated is never the way to feel about anything you do. Think positively, and positive things will happen! More than that, you can make them happen by taking a proactive approach. Sometimes it's not enough to just want to move up in a company and then go through the interview process. You may also need to demonstrate what you can do. For example, if you're seeking a promotion that requires a certain skill, perhaps the ability to create a sales presentation from scratch, go ahead and create one on your own. Then, show it to your superiors, giving them a clear idea of your talents and literally forcing them to take another look at what you can offer the company. Offer assistance to others in the department, make yourself visible. Also, when you interview for a possible promotion, bring along a list of your accomplishments, showing what you've achieved and why you have earned consideration for the higher level job. In other words, it's okay to sell yourself once in a while (provided you don't go overboard in your self-promotion efforts). You may be surprised to learn that your superiors will actually appreciate your initiative! I remember getting an opportunity to take on responsibility for a job I wanted to be promoted to. I decided to accept the opportunity and six months later I did receive the promotion.

Heroic Efforts

Going beyond the call of duty can increase your opportunities for career advancement.

Ever feel like you're just treading water at work, not really moving ahead as quickly as you would like? Sometimes, what you need to do is actually prove yourself worthy of advancement.

One of the best ways to put yourself in position for a promotion is to show initiative by making some sort of extra effort that everyone in your office—especially your boss—is sure to notice.

The following are some simple ideas for increasing your opportunities to move up the corporate ladder:

1. **Beat a deadline.** Almost every project in an office has a deadline attached to it. Try bringing a project to completion well ahead of its target date, demonstrating your willingness and ability to step up your performance if needed.

2. **Share your knowledge.** Be eager to assist a co-worker if they need help with something. This will show your superiors that you have the ability to take on a leadership role.

3. **Rescue the boss.** Chances are, you've witnessed your boss running around like a lunatic at the last moment, trying to prepare for an important meeting. Offer to help in any way you can, pointing out that with your assistance the boss will be better prepared for the meeting than if he or

she handled it alone. This will show your ability to work toward a specific goal as a team player.

4. **Be organized.** It's a fact that most managers take organization into account when considering someone for a promotion or even during their review. I learned many years ago while working as a customer service rep that it pays to be the person people can count on. The manager of the department was continually coming to me for help with a project. It seemed that I was the only one asked to do the extra work. When I asked her why she always chose me, the answer was, "I knew you could handle it." Six months later I was promoted to supervisor.

Dear Sharon,

I've used the [hanging] filing system for years and have found it to be very efficient and "user friendly." My boss has given me the task of designing and implementing a new, company-wide filing system and I must explain to the other secretaries why this is the easiest and most efficient way to file and retrieve. I don't know why—it just is! Can you give me an answer for them? Thanks, and by the way, I just discovered your site and have found what I've read so far quite helpful. Thanks again for your help.

Susan, Executive Assistant

Dear Susan,

What a great opportunity for you to shine. If you want to know why hanging filing is the BEST way to file you've certainly come to the right source. Are you aware that Pendaflex actually invented hanging filing? Studies have shown that individual files in a hanging system can be located three times faster than with other filing methods. Because hanging folders are suspended neatly on rails, the folders will not slump or sag, preventing tabs from getting blocked by other folders and also preventing papers from "sinking" into the dark reaches of the drawer bottom. Neatly aligned tabs also allow for "fingertip" retrieval of files; you simply skim your eyes and your fingers through the tabs to find what you need.

Appraising the Situation

Strategies for making sure your job evaluation works in your favor.

We've all been there: Your annual job-performance review is coming up and you're a little apprehensive. Sure, you've done a good job over the past year, and you've worked hard, but you're still not exactly sure how your boss will appraise your performance.

In most companies, and perhaps yours is no different, employees sit down with their bosses to discuss the employee's evaluation. Here are some tips to help you "nail" the appraisal interview and ensure a favorable review.

1. **Do a dry run.** Try to anticipate the kinds of things your boss will ask you and rehearse what your answers will be. For example, you will probably be asked to rate your job performance this year versus last year. Be ready to make comparisons that are favorable to your cause, such as "I have increased the projects I handle on a monthly basis by 15 percent."

2. **Ask for specifics.** Many bosses will fall into the trap of generalization, saying things such as "At times, you seem to lack initiative." Don't be afraid to ask the boss to expand on such a statement by suggesting that they point out specific examples. Then discuss the situation, always keeping the conversation positive so the boss realizes you plan to make improvements.

3. **Promote your attributes.** The appraisal process, from your point of view, should involve some salesmanship. In other words, don't hesitate to enumerate the benefits that you bring to the table. For instance, you might point out that you were originally hired to answer phones and file; however, you've also taken on the responsibility of producing departmental reports. Have a list prepared so you won't forget to make your point.

4. **Look to the future.** Perhaps more than anything else, the boss (and your company) is interested not so much in your past performance but what you can do in the months and

years to come. Your capacity to "grow into the job" and expand its importance will make you much more valuable to your employer. Be sure to make suggestions as to how you can enhance your role. For example, you could suggest that you coordinate training for new employees or work on developing cost-saving procedures for your department. Talk up your talents; your boss may not be aware of all of your past experience.

Get What's Coming to You

Tips to help you negotiate a higher salary.

Everyone wants to make the most money possible. After all, you work extremely hard and under tremendous pressure, especially now that the Internet and other technological advancements of recent years have made everything in the office move much faster.

Here are some tips I've compiled from human resources professionals at companies small and large that can help you receive the pay increase you know you deserve:

1. **Speak up.** Most people go into their annual job review, upon which pay raises are usually based, and simply sit back and accept everything their supervisor has to say— including the amount of salary increase. If you know you've done a great job in the past year, you owe it to

yourself to at least bring up the possibility that perhaps you are worth more than the company is offering. Most companies are willing to pay top dollar for the best talent.

2. **Aim high.** Of course, you can walk a fine line between being perceived as greedy and asking for the raise that you feel is owed to you. But did you know that most companies will offer significantly less money than is actually available? It's a fact. Most department managers will offer a raise that is actually below the figure they are authorized to approve—sometimes, as much as 2 or 3 percent lower! Therefore, it's probably a good idea to aim high in your asking price.

3. **Be realistic.** Although you want to put the largest possible raise in your pocket, you do not want to ask for a raise that is unattainable. In presenting your case, suggest a figure that "aims high" as mentioned above, yet is not completely outrageous. That way, you are more likely to walk away from your negotiations with a victory, even if it's not as great as you originally planned.

4. **Know when to back off.** In many instances, you can do all of the above, and still your supervisor will not budge. Instead, he or she will stick firmly to their guns and insist that you take the raise being offered—or leave it. In such a case, be sure not to push the envelope too far and label yourself as difficult. Many bosses will admire the fact that you spoke up for yourself and took the initiative to ask for more money. Yet, it's important to recognize that

sometimes there's simply no room in the budget to meet your higher salary demands, but since you've planted the seed, perhaps there will be next year.

5. **Document your achievements.** Getting a substantial raise can many times come down to proving your worth, in writing, to your boss. As you complete projects, keep track of them, taking special note of how they were completed on time, the extra duties you had to perform to meet a deadline and ways in which your efforts might have saved the company money. Then, when you sit down with your boss to discuss your raise, present the list of your achievements as ammunition in pleading your case.

6. **Be proactive.** At times, getting the raise you desire can mean taking on more responsibility. Rather than automatically accepting the increase you're presented with, offer to perform additional duties within your company or department, justifying a bigger increase.

7. **Get the facts.** Of course, every company is different, with budgets all their own. However, it may be important in your negotiations to know what other workers in similar fields are making throughout the marketplace. Average salaries for such positions as office administrator and executive assistant are listed in many publications each year (check with your library) so you can see for yourself if your compensation falls within industrywide averages.

8. **Be creative.** Your boss may be in total agreement with you, and yet the raise isn't there. Sometimes budgets and

company mandates make a raise impossible. There may be other solutions such as some time off, or tickets to the theater or dinner.

Attitude Adjustment

Stay positive and you'll stay in line for faster promotions.

Every department in every company seems to have at least one person who is always grumbling about something. Whether they're spouting off about having too much work, or that the boss is out to get them, or that the coffee isn't hot enough, these people can be annoying and can have a negative effect on their co-workers.

Fact is, people with bad attitudes are hurting themselves more than anyone else because in today's competitive business environment, companies want "team players" who can rise above the craziness and do a great job without complaining. It's the team players who get noticed in a company, and they're the ones that move ahead. Here are some tips to keep your attitude positive and put yourself in position to get faster promotions and receive bigger pay raises:

1. **Put on a happy face.** Granted, it can be difficult to remain cheerful when the stress of your job starts to get to you. However, it's very important not to let your emotions show,

especially if those emotions are negative. Smiling in the face of pressure exudes confidence and is a sure way to move up in your company.

2. **Keep it to yourself.** Airing your gripes about your company is certain to work against you. Resist the temptation to "get things off your mind" by complaining to co-workers, because it can quickly earn you a reputation as a "squeaky wheel."

3. **Be your own person.** Of course, adjusting your attitude to remain continually positive doesn't mean you can't speak your mind if something is really bothering you. The trick is how you go about it. For example, instead of angrily spewing out nasty comments about a certain work dilemma, calmly suggest ways to improve the situation.

Listen and Learn

Being a good listener can increase your chances for a promotion. Here's how.

As many office professionals proceed through their business careers and seek advancement, they are often under the impression that the two things that count most in gaining a promotion are working hard and getting noticed. While these are certainly critical elements in business success, there's a third skill that people sometimes overlook—the ability to listen.

Recent studies have shown that business leaders and other people who are instrumental in the hiring and promotion process rank "good listening" among the top five skills they want from their employees. Furthermore, nearly 75 percent of business executives in the Fortune 500 group of companies consider the ability to listen "extremely important."

It all makes perfect sense. To do your job well you must be able to listen to direction from your boss, then execute that direction in the best way possible. Failure to listen can lead to miscommunication, and, in business, that can mean losses in the thousands or millions of dollars.

The bottom line? Being a good listener will help you avoid mistakes that can derail your career and also allow you to absorb as much knowledge as possible, to learn more about your company, its industry, its markets. Then utilize that knowledge to eventually impress your superiors with your actions and climb the corporate ladder.

Here are several traits that describe a good listener:

1. **Be patient while someone else is talking,** particularly if the person is a business superior. Avoid the urge to interrupt.
2. **Maintain continual eye contact.** This demonstrates that you are paying attention to the speaker.
3. **While listening, use body language** that shows you are interested in what is being said. For instance, when the speaker makes a key point, lean forward as if you're striving to hear each word better.

4. **When the person you are talking to is finished speaking and it's your turn to speak, try whenever possible (without overdoing it) to restate** or summarize their thoughts and weave them into your own comments. This shows not only that you're a good listener but that you also understand what is being said.

Leading Questions

Have what it takes to be the boss?
Ask yourself these five questions.

Ever wonder if you have what it takes to be the boss? Although there are countless aspects and criteria that can be used to measure the abilities of a supervisor to lead successfully, I offer five basic questions for you to ponder to help determine if you're management material:

1. **Can you delegate?** Chances are, while in a nonsupervisory position, you've become accustomed to a hands-on approach of doing the work yourself. As a boss, you'll need to step back a notch and rely on your associates to control the "nuts and bolts" of a project while you manage the big picture.

2. **Can you motivate?** Being a successful leader means bringing out the best in the people who work for you. You must be able to get to know the strengths (and recognize the

weaknesses) of your team members in order to guide them and encourage them to new levels of success.

3. **Can you mediate?** As the boss, it's likely you'll occasionally be called upon to intervene in a disagreement among your associates. Be sure you can remain neutral, being careful not to take sides, while finding a solution that will benefit your team as a whole.

4. **Can you tolerate?** Along with the increase in salary and importance that come with being a leader, there also comes the pressure of managing such details as perform-  ance reviews, departmental budgets, assignments for your team members and many other things. At the same time, you must also meet the demands of your own boss. Translation? You'll usually find yourself in the middle, wearing the dual hats of boss and team member— and that can require the patience to take things in stride.

5. **Can you demonstrate?** Another vital skill in being a successful boss is the ability to lead by example. In other words, practice what you preach among associates, whether it be your full commitment to each project, your honesty, or any other way you conduct yourself in the office. In the long run, you'll nurture the trust of your employees and gain their respect.

Power Trip

So, you've just moved up to management. Here's how to be a good boss.

Congratulations. You have worked extremely hard and the promotion you've been waiting for has finally come through. Now, you'll be in charge of a small department all by yourself, with six people reporting to you.

You have all the experience you need to make your new job something special. You also have good people working for you, but it's very important that you're able to motivate them—and keep them happy—in order to run your busy department efficiently and productively.

Here are some tips for being a good boss and getting the most out of the people who work for you:

1. **Hear what they say.** Nobody likes working for a faceless boss who sits back and communicates only by memorandum. Schedule informal talk sessions where you and your new staff can interact and exchange ideas on a regular basis. And remember, communication works both ways, so be a good listener.

2. **Keep your promises.** If you say you will do something for one of your employees, for instance give them a raise, then make sure you follow through. If you repeatedly make promises to your staff and then fail to deliver on the

promises, you will quickly lose credibility as well as the respect of your staff.

3. **Show gratitude.** When employees do a good job or when they perform a task that is over and above what is expected, let them know about it by praising them. Words of thanks and encouragement can go a long way in getting employees to work to their full potential.

4. **Avoid intimidation.** For the most part, human nature dictates that people will react negatively to scare tactics. Of course, at times you may need to be stern with staff members who do not perform to your expectations. However, continually "being in the face" of your employees will probably turn them off—and turn them on you.

5. **Be goal oriented with each employee.** It's imperative for each of your staff members to know exactly what their role is in your department or organization and exactly what is expected of them. Don't hesitate to set goals for each individual employee and be certain to regularly discuss these goals with them to review the employee's progress.

Naturally, there are many, many other strategies for being a good boss and as you "grow into the job" you'll discover what works best for you and your associates. But if you adhere to the basic approaches discussed above and build from there, you'll be well on your way to being successful in your new management position!

Today's workforce is constantly being bombarded with layoffs and changes. The next few articles will deal with the art of looking for a new job or career.

The Upside of Downsizing

Layoffs can be traumatic, but they can also expand your career opportunities.

In this era of mergers and acquisitions, which can involve huge conglomerates as well as tiny firms, one thing sometimes get misplaced in the shuffle—jobs.

When one company acquires another, the outcome can often mean downsizing or elimination of job positions that may be redundant as the staffs of two companies join forces.

Of course, being downsized can be scary and is often unexpected, but it can also broaden career opportunities by paving the way for you to move on to bigger and better things. A disappointment can lead to an opportunity.

To help ensure that you give your career every opportunity to expand, here are some suggestions in the event that you are downsized:

1. **Take your contacts file with you.** Getting a great new job can be all about knowing people, so if you are suddenly laid off, be sure to take along a list of people you've done business with previously.
2. **Make a list of your accomplishments.** This is not

intended to replace a résumé, but employers find it easier to hire someone who comes prepared with a quick-reference overview of what they can bring to the table.

3. **Set high standards.** Granted, at times it can be tough to land a job, particularly when the economy is stagnant. But that doesn't necessarily mean you have to accept just any job. Go after the job you really want, keeping in mind that if you start looking with high expectations you have a better chance of reaching them.

4. **Negotiate.** If you get an offer for a new job, don't be afraid to negotiate the salary and perks (such as vacation time). It is likely that your potential employer will be willing to offer you more in order to get you on board.

Time to Move On?

How do you know when it's time to look for a new job?

Although you may feel hesitant about looking for a new job at the moment, chances are that one day you'll be considering whether you should leave your present employer and move on.

With that in mind, you should know how to recognize the signs that you are ready to change jobs. That way, you'll be better prepared for the move when the opportunity arises.

The following are some tell-tale signals that it's time to start searching for a new job:

1. **You see a lack of advancement potential.** According to many job placement experts, if you have not been promoted within your present department or company for at least five years, provided you want to advance, chances are you might want to look to another company to receive the higher position, and bigger salary, you seek.

2. **You no longer feel challenged.** Many people thrive on being able to handle increasing responsibilities. If you're one of those people, and the work you're doing no longer seems up to your capabilities, perhaps you can find the challenges you want at another company.

3. **You want more recognition.** Over time, some corporate workers may feel as though they're being taken for granted, that what they do is not appreciated enough. Certainly, this can be true, particularly in larger companies where the contributions of individuals can sometimes get lost in the immense structure and bureaucracy. One suggestion would be to look for a position at a smaller firm, one that you will not only grow with, but one at which you can also make a significant difference in the growth itself.

4. **You realize you simply need revival.** Becoming complacent is something that can negatively affect many people. Yet, a large percentage of people are not even aware that they're just going through the motions at work. Obtaining a new job can result in a whole new outlook—revitalizing both your professional life as well as the way you approach life in general.

Of course, there are many other signs that suggest it's time to move on to a new job, many more than I have room for here. Maybe the most important thing to remember is that your needs are unique to you, and, if possible, you might want to seek a job that best fits your traits instead of the other way around.

Put Yourself Out There

Looking for a new job? Here's how to market yourself most effectively.

In order to enhance your opportunities for landing your "dream job," it's important that you market your talents in a way that will give you the most opportunities.

Here are just a few of the many strategies for getting the word out about yourself and what you can bring to a prospective employer.

1. **Develop a strong résumé.** Naturally, this is the first place most people start in their job search. However, it's imperative to avoid the trap of simply listing your job experience and your titles. To make yourself more attractive to potential employers, also use your resume to describe what you've accomplished in the positions you've held, citing specific ways, for example, of how you helped your current and past employers grow their businesses, or run their operations more productively. And you should always keep your resume current.

2. **Post your resume, everywhere.** It's not enough anymore to just send your resume out in the mail. Today, you also need to put your qualifications online by posting your resume on Web sites specifically devoted to placing job candidates. Employers are continually checking such Web postings to find the right candidates.

3. **Network.** One of the best ways to find a new job is to interact with "people who know people." Perhaps you have a friend who works at a company that is looking for someone with your talents. It's also a good idea to join a networking group, which includes people who meet regularly and discuss ways in which they can assist each other in their business lives.

4. **Recognize your strengths.** Before you get ready to actually sit down with a potential employer in an interview, review your own attributes. Ask yourself, *What do I do best?* and when you do go on the interview, try to steer the conversation around to your strong points.

5. **Do your research.** In targeting companies you want to work for, be certain to get to know as much as you can about those companies. Then, when you're at the job interview, display your knowledge about the company you're visiting. This will greatly impress your prospective boss and he or she will view you as a person who has taken the initiative to learn what the company needs and what the job position entails.

You, Only Better

Five tips for creating résumés that enhance your image and your job prospects.

Usually, as you well know, the competition for good positions at top companies is fierce, and it's imperative that your resume really stands out. After all, for most job seekers, the resume is the very first impression that is made on a prospective employer.

The following are five smart and simple ideas for looking your best on paper and ensuring that your résumé communicates the right message:

1. **Be chronological.** Presenting your job experience with the most recent position listed first is an age-old approach, and it's one that's still highly effective. Most employers want to know what you've done lately, so they can translate those skills and background into the job needs they have right now.

2. **Tout your accomplishments, specifically.** Instead of just listing that you were in charge of the "Northeast market" for a previous employer, state actual achievements you reached while in the position, such as sales increases for your company because of you, promotions gained, awards won, efficiencies increased in your department, and so on.

3. **Avoid negatives and excuses.** Never list in your résumé the reasons why you are no longer working at a particular company, such as "because of a hostile takeover," or "the

boss had an agenda and would not promote me." Always be positive with everything you present in a résumé. You do not want to be labeled as a complainer.

4. **Get a second opinion.** Once you have your résumé just about ready, ask a friend or relative to take a look at it and provide any ideas or constructive criticism they may have. Another set of eyes could be very valuable in fine-tuning a résumé.

5. **Be selective.** It's tempting to mass-mail your résumé to every classified job listing you see in the paper or online. However, this is not the best approach. Read the ads carefully, matching your skills and experience, instead of wasting your time targeting jobs you don't want or have no chance of getting. As an extra added touch if you are mailing your résumé, why not use a portfolio. It shows initiative and commitment on your part.

The Story of You

How to sell yourself in a job interview when an employer says, "Tell me about your background." An inside look at questions often asked in an interview and how best to answer them.

Anyone who has ever been on an interview knows that most likely, after the initial chit-chat, the employer will eventually get around to asking you to describe yourself beyond what appears on your résumé. Usually, the employer will begin this process with a simple phrase: "Tell me about yourself." This is your cue to really shine, your opportunity to show your potential boss that you have what they're looking for!

Here are some simple tips to help make certain that when you're asked to describe yourself and your background, you go about it the right way:

1. **Preparation.** An interview is as much a conversation as it is a question and answer session. So you must be prepared to discuss not just your credentials but how those credentials can help your prospective employer. This requires (as mentioned previously in this guide) doing your homework by researching the company and/or the position beforehand to determine exactly what the job will consist of.

2. **Rehearse.** Although you don't want your answer to sound like you're reading a script, you want to be sure that the facts and the "meat" of your answer are readily available when the time comes to describe what you have to offer. Although it seems a logical thing to do, you would be surprised how many people actually go into a job interview with little or no preparation.

3. **Make a logical progression.** The interviewer is interested in reviewing your past and how it led to where you are today. Be careful not to jump around chronologically, instead describe your background in a timeline fashion that progresses from past to present.

4. **Keep it business, all business.** Of course, your family is important, however a prospective employer is not really interested in that—at least not during the first interview. When you're asked to describe yourself, be sure to review your business skills, emphasizing strengths and accomplishments that relate specifically to work. Do not discuss your family, friends, hobbies or personal life (and legally the interviewer cannot ask about personal information that is not job related).

5. **Relate to your audience.** During your description of your work experience and attributes, it's important to discuss what you can bring to the employer. Before going to the interview, read about the company, learn their business as best you can, and then talk about how your background can help that company in the specific position you are applying for.

6. **Stay short and sweet.** Remember that the person interviewing you is probably quite busy. So when asked to describe yourself, be concise and to the point, not long winded. As a rule of thumb, your answer should be about two to three minutes long. Also be polite and use a friendly tone of voice at all times.

7. **Packaging.** How you present yourself can be as important in a hiring decision as what's on your resume or in your background. You've heard the expression "dress for success," and it still holds true. Think carefully about the image you want to present. If possible, visit the company

discreetly prior to your interview to see how other workers dress. Remember, your prospective employer has a
particular image in mind when filling an open position,
and you'll have a definite edge if you fit that image.

8. **Confidence.** Hold your head high when you enter the room,
and offer a firm handshake. Also maintain eye contact.

9. **Congeniality.** Above all, be yourself. Let your personality
show. Keep in mind that your prospective boss is thinking
ahead about what it would be like to work with you and
how you would interact with co-workers.

Here are three of the more common things that employers ask
a job seeker, along with some tips about how you should best for-
mulate your answers:

1. **Why are you interested in our company?** Think of this
question as not only easy, but also very opportune. Be
careful to avoid answering with the obvious by saying
something like "Because I need a job," or, "Because the
benefits are really good." Instead, enthusiastically discuss
three or four aspects of the company that interest you and
that also serve as compliments for your prospective
employer. For example, when asked what you like about
the company, you could say something like, "I feel that the
way in which the company is positioned in today's marketplace will allow for extensive growth, both for the
company itself and for me professionally."

2. **What are your major strengths?** Here is where you can expand upon what's written in your resume and cite specific examples about what you have brought to the table for previous employers and what you can do for the company you're now trying to join. Avoid generalities such as "I'm a people person" and instead focus on actual circumstances, such as "My versatile abilities to interact smoothly with associates as well as superiors enables me to contribute on many levels throughout the company."

3. **What is your major weakness?** Now, you really have a chance to look good. Sure, some people are frightened by this question, but why? This is a great opportunity to turn the tables and make something potentially negative into a real positive. For example, you could say "I sometimes work too late, and I tend to worry over the details of my job, taking responsibility to make certain that every project is completed in the best way." My favorite is "Sometimes I am too enthusiastic and I have a difficult time waiting for the right moment to share my ideas."

Dear Sharon:

Do you have any tips for filing job search information so I can easily keep track of job search efforts? Thank you.

Graeme, Software Developer

Dear Graeme,

I have two suggestions for you: (1) Use Oxford® index cards and (2) Oxford® card guides to neatly organize your job search efforts. For instance, you could use a different index card for each job prospect, writing down such information as the date you went on your interview, key contacts, follow-up, etc. Then, create a file of index cards with sections of the file separated by card guides. The guides are available preprinted with alphabetical, daily (1–31) or monthly tabs, making it simple for you to quickly access your job search information and pull a card about each job prospect when needed. You want to keep track of the dates you send your résumés, thank you letters, etc.

Hello, It's Me

Tips for creating cover letters that best introduce you to prospective employers.

Much the same as when you enter a room at a party, presenting your résumé should be done in a certain style. The presentation of a mailed résumé is accomplished by a cover letter, and it's imperative that the letter be compelling and that it entices the reader to actually open the résumé to find out more about you. Here are five simple ideas for ensuring that your cover letters are more appealing:

1. **Make things personal.** Never send out a "format" letter that sounds and looks like every other one a prospective employer has ever seen. Instead take the time to find out a little about the company you're writing to, then say why you're interested in working there and how your qualifications could be of value to the company in a specific way.

2. **Announce your intentions early on.** Recruiters, HR people and department managers are inundated with thousands of cover letters, all of which they have to weed through. Don't waste their time beating around the bush; tell them right away why you're writing. Example, "I am responding to your need for an office supervisor and I

feel that my experience and qualifications are just what your company is looking for."

3. **Give a few highlights.** Ultimately, gaining a job interview is a three-step process: you want the reader to first open your cover letter; then go on to evaluate your résumé; then contact you to schedule the interview itself. In your letter, point out a few key facts about yourself that are spelled out in the résumé, such as how you've helped your company build sales by 24 percent, or how you've helped cut costs at your present employer by 16 percent.

4. **Differentiate yourself.** Select a few key items from your résumé that you feel set you apart from other applicants and mention them in the cover letter. For instance, you might say that not only have you managed your company's filing system, you have created a more efficient method of organizing customer files that has saved your company approximately $550 in administrative expenses over the past year.

5. **Be action oriented.** Always make certain to conclude your cover letter with a definitive desire to take the next step. State that you are available immediately for a personal interview, and don't forget to provide applicable information about where you can be reached (phone number, e-mail address, cell phone number, etc.). Prospective employers will like the fact that you are demonstrating a proactive approach toward getting the job; this shows right off the bat that you are motivated.

If the résumé gets you an interview, always remember to send a thank you letter as a follow up after the interview.

Making the Rounds

The importance of networking and using business events to advance your career.

Have you ever asked yourself why some people always seem to get ahead in the business world and others don't? Sure, what you know is important, but who you know can also be a major factor in helping you find a better job with more pay.

It's called networking, and it involves interacting with as many people as possible in order to advance your business career and theirs. The concept behind networking is quite straightforward: "Spread the word" about yourself. Whether you're looking for a new job or trying to sign up a new account, the more people you meet the more opportunities will come your way.

Of course, discretion is important in networking. If you are looking for a new job you don't want your boss knowing that you're job-hunting. However, don't hesitate to speak with other people in your life—people that you may not have considered as potentially able to help you advance your career. Your friends, neighbors and relatives are great networking sources. Perhaps one of these people has heard about a job opening at the company they work for.

Here are tips to help you network most effectively:

1. **Mingle, and mingle some more.** At parties and other gatherings, strike up a conversation about your work, engaging the other person to share information about their job or company.

2. **Expand from within.** Start with your own circle of friends and immediate acquaintances. Most likely, these people will be eager to help you.

3. **Pass out your business cards.** Don't hesitate to give out cards whenever the opportunity arises. You never know.

4. **Be prepared.** Before you attend the event, know what you want to accomplish. If you feel that the company picnic will provide just the right relaxed venue to approach your boss about a new idea you have, then practice beforehand how you will broach the subject.

5. **Dress appropriately.** Even if the event will be held at a nightclub, that's no reason to wear your slinkiest party dress. Keep in mind, the underlying theme of the event might be business related.

6. **Make an entrance.** As with any party, the way to get noticed is to arrive fashionably late (if possible). Advancing your career can have as much to do with creating a presence for yourself as it does with your accomplishments.

7. **Follow up.** If you attend a holiday party at the vice president's home, take the time to drop him or her a line thanking them for inviting you. This is not only good manners, it

will help keep you in the forefront of their mind when promotion time rolls around.

8. **Join a group.** Networking clubs are everywhere, and they
make it easy for people to get together on a regular basis and
share information about how they can assist one another in
advancing their careers.

There was a time when networking would make me run for the
nearest closet and hide. I would go to a social engagement, find
the most comfortable chair—hopefully it was by the chips—and
stay there until someone approached me first. Only recently I had
to give an opening speech to eight hundred and fifty people. I had
five minutes and at the end I was looking for more. I was thrilled
to get this message in my e-mail the following week. "I did not get
a chance to tell you that I really enjoyed your speech at the
Annual Business Meeting luncheon. It was very touching. I
noticed people listening with intent and with over eight hundred
organizers in the room, I know that is quite a task." It just takes
practice, and, believe me, I did, to anyone who would listen.

CHAPTER 12

PRESERVING THE ENVIRONMENT

Playing Your Part

Natural resources have never been more precious, and the need to continually preserve them is vital. You can do your part, every day, to help protect the environment for future generations. I thought that it was important to include a chapter on some smart approaches to recycling.

Thinking Globally

Ways to make your office more environmentally friendly.

Preserving Earth's natural resources is everyone's responsibility, and one of the best places to start is in your office.

Here are eight ways in which you can make your office more "Earth friendly" every day:

1. **Always** turn off your copy machine at night to save energy.

2. **Photocopy on both sides** to reduce paper consumption. The average office worker uses a massive two hundred sheets of paper a day.

3. **Instead of creating a bunch of paper memos,** use your computer to deliver e-mail messages to co-workers.

4. **If interoffice memos are necessary,** try to route the same memo from person to person, rather than making numerous copies.

5. **Take discarded office paper home** for use as telephone message pads and shopping lists, or for the kids to use as drawing paper.

6. **Use refillable-ink pens** instead of disposable ones (you'd be surprised how little things like this can ease the burden on overcrowded landfills).

7. **Urge** your cafeteria to use regular plates, not paper ones. And avoid taking unnecessary handfuls of napkins.

8. **Always** recycle aluminum soda and juice cans and bottles.

How Good-Natured Are You?

Is your office preserving natural resources?

Not too long ago most people took nature and the world around us for granted, believing that such resources as clean air, plentiful water and thriving forests would always be there. Of course, we've all learned that these resources are indeed precious and they must be preserved to ensure that they will be available for our children and grandchildren.

Here are four easy steps that you and your co-workers can take to make your office "better natured" and more environmentally friendly:

1. **Use recycled filing supplies.** These are products, such as EarthWise® brand file folders and index cards and Pendaflex® 100% Recycled Hanging Folders, that are made from recycled fibers and contain maximum amounts of post-consumer material. When you use recycled filing supplies, you're doing a vital part in helping to preserve natural resources.

2. **Preserve electricity whenever possible.** Be sure to turn out the lights when you leave the office for extended periods, such as during lunch time and at the end of the day.

3. **Be thrifty with heat and air conditioning.** A climate-controlled office can use up a lot of power, which requires natural resources to generate. Although most office workers don't have direct control over the temperature in the

building (it's usually the responsibility of the building maintenance staff), you can nonetheless contact the operators of your building and request that thermostats are more moderately controlled to optimize heating and cooling efficiency. Think about it: Just by wearing a sweater at work in the winter instead of turning the heat all the way up, you could be making a valuable difference in the preservation of Earth's resources.

4. **Commute with someone else.** If you drive to work, consider a carpool. This will not only save gas (and money), it will also lessen the amount of exhaust that goes into the atmosphere. At the same time, it will help to reduce the amount of traffic on the road, and that could speed your commute!

What Goes Around Comes Around

How to set up an office paper recycling program.

Protecting the environment for future generations is one of the most vital things each of us can do, and it's everyone's responsibility—particularly people who work in an office and create presentations, reports, letters and other paper-intensive documents.

One of the best ways to be environmentally friendly in your office is to actively recycle your office paper. It's easier than you might imagine to create your own office recycling program; here's all you do:

1. **Appoint someone in your office to be the "recycling coordinator,"** and rotate the responsibility to get everyone involved on a continuing basis.

2. **Place individual "paper collection" trays or boxes throughout your office,** near the copy machine, close to each workstation, and so on.

3. **Set up a large, central collection box** and periodically (perhaps at the end of each week) empty the contents of each individual collection receptacle into the central collection box.

4. **Arrange for your company's or building's maintenance staff to periodically transfer contents** of the collection box to a temporary storage area.

5. **Contact a reputable recyclable waste dealer** or paper recycling firm and coordinate a weekly schedule for them to pick up the paper you collect. (Many waste dealers pay for recyclable paper, so your office recycling program will easily pay for itself!)

Earth to You

**Calling all environmentally friendly people:
choose recycled filing products wisely.**

When filing your office and home-office documents, you can play an important role in conserving precious natural resources by using recycled filing supplies, but not just any recycled filing supplies. The key is to look for products that have maximum amounts of post-consumer content.

Now, you may be asking yourself, what does "post-consumer content" mean? By definition, the term refers to material that has been used, discarded and then reused to make other products. This can make a very positive difference to the environment in two ways: Not only are natural resources conserved, the amount of waste that goes into overflowing landfills is also decreased.

So, what can you do? When selecting recycled filing products for your office or home office (or if someone at your company does the purchasing of filing supplies, show them this article) check the package for post-consumer content. If you do not see any reference to this content, chances are the product does not contain a high percentage of post-consumer waste.

EarthWise® Recycled Filing Supplies have maximum post-consumer content. In fact, EarthWise brand was the first to exceed revised EPA guidelines for environmental filing products.

And you can choose from a complete line of EarthWise hanging file folders, interior folders, regular file folders, partition folders, slash pockets, index cards and expanding products. In addition to doing something good for the Earth, you can also be sure that you're getting top quality—the same quality and performance as non-recycled filing supplies!

Remember, choose recycled filing products wisely by insisting on maximum post-consumer content. Ask your office products supplier or retailer today about EarthWise Recycled Filing Supplies.

Dear Sharon,

When my filing cabinet filled up I started archiving papers in boxes and shelves in my office. I am out of room and the amount of paper is overwhelming. What is a good way to approach moving some of the papers to a recycle bin?

Rebecca, Scientist

Dear Rebecca,

I'm happy to hear that you are recycling your used office paper. As I'm sure you and all our readers already know, it's important that everyone who works in an office is aware of the need to preserve natural resources and protect the environment for future generations. Here's all you have to do to set up an easy-to-use paper recycling approach for your office: Simply place "paper collection" trays or boxes throughout your office, near the copy machine, close to each workstation, next to the computer printer and so on. Then, periodically (probably once a week) arrange for your building's maintenance staff to transfer the contents to a temporary storage area where it can be picked up by a recyclable waste dealer. Oh, and here's another tidbit: Many waste dealers will actually pay for high-quality, office-type recyclable paper!

CHAPTER 13

ORGANIZING FOR HOME AND SCHOOL

How to Balance It All

Many of us struggle with balancing home and work and how to keep it all together. For me it was routines that kept me in balance. Here are some articles specific to home life to help you get through the day-to-day challenges in life.

Clip, Save, Organize

Smart ideas for keeping track of coupons.

Many of us may not realize it, but there are people who save thousands of dollars each year by clipping and using coupons that offer savings on virtually anything you can think of—food, clothing, entertainment, tires, cosmetics, cleaning supplies. The list goes on and on.

The challenge is not finding these coupons in newspapers, magazines and mailers. It's organizing them so that you can utilize them in a timely fashion and take advantage of the savings that are offered.

Here are just a few smart ways to store, manage and access the coupons you clip:

1. **Use an actual filing system.** Many people just throw their coupons into a drawer haphazardly, never to be seen again. Some great suggestions for filing your coupons include using an expandable file.

2. **Arrange by date.** Almost every coupon has an expiration date, and, of course, if the coupon is not used in time it becomes worthless. Arrange your coupons so that the dates that are coming close to expiration are in the front of your coupon filing system.

3. **Remove outdated coupons regularly.** On a periodic basis, check through your coupons to find and take out the ones that have expired. These coupons are just taking up space and will also make your "live" coupons more difficult to find.

4. **Show restraint.** Many times, the urge is to clip every possible coupon you might remotely be interested in. Try to avoid doing this. Instead, clip and save only the coupons you think you'll actually use.

Class Actions

Attention teachers: here are four ways to better organize your classroom.

Teaching is an art all to itself. The ability to impart knowledge to young people and prepare them for success in their future lives is among the most critical talents anyone can have.

Perhaps you're a teacher yourself, or you know someone who teaches and maybe, just maybe, you could use a few easy ideas to help make life in the classroom a little more organized.

Here are four suggestions:

1. **Use color, as I have mentioned many times before.** For example, student files can be much simpler to reference if different colors are assigned to the files. Color creates a visual signal that distinguishes one file from another. Another choice includes file folders, which also come in many colors. You might even want to color-match the file folders to the colors of notebooks, or the colors of book covers, for enhanced organizing efficiency.

2. **Designate "organize" time.** Kids will be kids and most of the time, kids will be messy—if you let them. Set aside a few minutes each day during which students should organize their desks, their personal belongings and anything else that may be cluttering their classroom lives. The teacher should also utilize this time to organize his or her own desk.

3. **Take advantage of the walls.** Many classrooms are constantly adorned with decorations or with recent work that students have done. And that's great. However, walls can also provide plenty of extra space for staying organized. If shelves are already on the walls, use them to neatly store such things as books, binders and other reference materials—rather than taking up valuable room on a desk. If shelves are not in place, perhaps the school's custodial staff should be asked to install them, enabling many more possibilities for productive organization.

4. **Label things.** Self-stick labels are a terrific strategy for identifying and organizing schools supplies, cabinet drawers, storage closets, computer equipment, and a host of other items and places in a classroom. Electronic label-makers print great-looking, high-visibility labels in many colors at the touch of a button—making them an ideal complement to every classroom.

Store More, Search Less

Five ideas for organizing and finding things in your garage or workshop.

For many families, the garage is not only the place where the car occasionally gets parked. It's the place where everything from tools to toys gets thrown, often just to get them out of the house.

And then there's the workshop, which was supposed to be your husband's "fix-it" shop but eventually became buried in masses of castaways from every other room in your home.

Alas, both the garage and the workshop in many homes have become completely and utterly disorganized. Here are some ideas for solving the problem:

1. **Use baby food jars.** No, you don't have to have babies in your house. You can actually purchase empty jars at almost any home center. These compact containers are ideal for storing nails, screws, hooks, nuts, bolts and other small fasteners. To make things even more organized and easier to find, use an electronic labeler to create self-stick labels that identify what's in the jars.

2. **Store paperwork in binders.** In the workshop, instruction manuals for power tools can be three-hole punched and put into ring binders for referencing whenever needed. Or, use sheet protectors—just put the instructions into the sheet protectors (which are prepunched for use with three-ring binders) and place into binders. Here's another suggestion you probably never considered: Store sandpaper in binders! Simply punch holes in the sandpaper and insert into a ring binder.

3. **Put up pegboards.** They've been around forever and that's because they work! You can purchase a pegboard (which has holes already in it and allows for hanging various items on hooks placed into the holes) at any

hardware store. Hammers, pliers and wrenches can be hung for easy retrieval whenever you need them. In addition to pegboards for hand tools, use the walls in your garage to hang up shovels, garden implements and other larger tools—as well as bicycles—keeping them off the floor where they can be tripped upon.

4. **Identify cans of paint.** Did you just finish a painting project but didn't use all the paint? Keep it for another project. Before storing, put some paint from the inside of the can on the top lid. You'll always know what color the paint is without having to remove the lid.

5. **Utilize old cabinetry.** Have you recently replaced those old cabinets in your kitchen, or are you putting a new medicine cabinet in your bathroom? Don't throw away the old cabinets, instead, put them on the wall in your garage or workshop. They'll provide a perfect, quick-find place for storing cans of automotive fluid, repair manuals, garden nozzles, hoses, work gloves and many other things.

Keeping It in Balance

Work, family, your life—tips for balancing it all.

If anybody says it's easy, they have no idea. We're talking what may be the most difficult job a person can have. Actually, it's two jobs rolled into one—that of being a working parent.

Often awake at the crack of dawn and not able to relax even for a moment until well into the wee hours of the night, parents who also hold down career-oriented work positions are routinely challenged beyond belief. Yet, they're not alone.

In fact, there are millions of moms and dads who work on a full-time basis and somehow manage to successfully handle the demands of school-age children and a hectic family life.

The following are a few tips that may assist you in creating some balance between your work, your family and your life in general.

1. **Utilize technology.** Time is perhaps the most formidable enemy to the working parent. Give yourself more of it by taking full advantage of online bill paying. Other suggestions include: e-mailing instead of playing "telephone tag," instant messaging and keeping track of appointments with a "palm" or handheld device.

2. **Plan ahead.** Obviously, you have to make the most of what little time you have, and that can often mean being prepared in advance. Some ideas include: making your kids' school lunches and packing their backpacks the night before rather than scurrying the next morning, also putting their clothes out the night before, and getting yourself showered and dressed before the kids awake. You could also take some time on the weekends to make dinners ahead of time, then store them in the refrigerator for heating up during your busy work week.

3. **Stick to routines.** For example, (if you can get them to agree) have your kids do their homework at the same time each evening and be sure they go to bed at the same time. When routines are in place, children know what to expect. Also establish a routine for yourself—when you will have breakfast, what time you will leave for work each day, etc. As a working mother or father, you have enough variables to worry about in your life, so it's important to try and keep some things the same.

4. **Maintain up-to-date records.** Doctors' appointments, bills that are due, letters that need response, keeping track of the schedules of each person in your family—these are all things that need to be organized. One way is to use smartly designed filing products, such as the Pendaflex® Project Sorter (product # 50995), which comes complete with ten color-coded sorting tabs and a color-matched index for filing and finding family paperwork within categorized sections.

5. **Set aside "family time."** Yes, it's easier said than done, but it's essential, especially to your kids. Insist that—despite soccer practice, school plays, babysitting jobs and a myriad of other distractions—the family must sit down to dinner together at least a few times every week.

Child's Play

Five simple ways to keep the kids' toys neat and orderly.

Any family that includes young children has undoubtedly fought the battle of the "messy toys monster," where everything from action figures to plush animals are continuously strewn all over the house. Try these five ideas for organizing toys in your home:

1. **Under-bed storage.** Toys that are played with frequently, such as favorite dolls, can be stored in bins or boxes underneath the child's bed. It's space that would otherwise probably not be used, providing extra room that you likely need. Specially designed slide-out storage units are available specifically for under-bed use.

2. **Choose versatile organizing accessories.** File crates are a good example because they offer so much more versatility than just being able to organize filed records. They are lightweight, with handles for easily transporting toys from one location to another. What's more, they're stackable with an interlocking design to make the most of vertical space. Another good example is the Oxford® DecoSorter™ Step Rack, which is ideal for storing and organizing computer games and music CDs. Step Rack features six different compartments with dividers for arranging items into categories.

The stepped design makes it easy to access everything.

3. **Keep the boxes that toys came in.** Puzzles and board games typically contain many pieces, which can get lost in a hurry. Sometimes, parents are quick to toss away the original boxes and substitute bags with twist-ties or other less-durable storage options. Usually, the boxes that puzzles and games come in are fairly strong, able to survive constant use. To further ensure that nothing is lost, have your kids secure the box with a rubber band after each play session.

4. **Use shelves.** The walls in your home can complement closets and toy chests very nicely. Designate a separate shelf for different toy categories. Example: put art and drawing toys on one shelf and small electronic toys on another. To make your shelf approach even more efficient, use a labeler to create self-stick labels that identify each shelf. This helps assure that the right toys are put back in the right place. For smaller children who cannot read, you could also use stickers with pictures on them.

5. **Make donations.** As your children outgrow certain toys, consider donating them to charities. As sentimental as some toys can become, they'll probably just collect dust eventually. Besides, a needy child might truly enjoy the toy and put it to very good use.

Dear Sharon,

I have trouble keeping the kids' toys organized. My children are four and six and it seems that I am always picking up after them, not to mention the clutter around the house.

Marie, Exhausted Mom

Dear Marie,

It's never too early to start training your children to be organized. I would get colorful containers such as crates or bins and assign each of your children their own set of colors. Store toys and games by category and match up to a specific color. Create a game to see if they can match the item to the correct container. Give out stickers as an acknowledgement every time they get it right. Keep this up for a month and cleaning up their toys will become second nature. It takes less than a month to create a habit.

Garden Variety

Diverse ideas for organizing garden tools.

When summer is upon us, for millions of people that means it's time to re-activate our green thumbs and get down and dirty in the garden. But first, you should know about some simple ideas for organizing those all-important gardening tools you'll be utilizing over the next several months.

Here are some suggestions:

1. **Store the tools you use most often in a wagon.** That way, you'll be sure to keep them together for finding when needed, plus, you'll have a ready-to-use mobile vehicle for taking your gardening tools from the shed or garage to the garden itself.

2. **Reuse an old kitchen cabinet.** Have a cabinet lying around after your kitchen renovation? Get more mileage out of it by giving it a second life as a gardening tool organizer. Even if you don't have an old cabinet, you could buy one relatively cheaply at any home improvement store. Hang the cabinet where you can get to it easily and devote the entire cabinet solely to your gardening implements.

3. **Put up a pegboard in your garage, storage space, closet or basement.** Pegboards are great for all kinds of tools, especially small garden shovels, clippers, pruners and

other items. Always remember to hang the tools back up on the pegboard after use, and if possible, put them on the same peg each time for faster locating of the tools you need.

4. **Get yourself a fishing tackle box with a lid.** These boxes, which almost always have handles on them for convenient carrying, are ideal for storing gardening gloves, seed packets, those little markers that identify your plants and many other easy-to-misplace things.

Stuff the Bird, Not Your Cabinets

Five tips for organizing your kitchen, just in time for the holidays.

The holiday season always seems to come so quickly. Obviously, it's a busy time of year, particularly if you're planning on hosting family and friends for dinner.

One of the ways to help make certain that your holiday season is less stressful is to get your kitchen organized and keep it that way.

Here are five smart ideas:

1. **Install sliding shelves inside base cabinets.** "Sliding" shelving kits, specially designed for use inside kitchen cabinets, are available at most home centers. These types of shelves glide on rollers and they are usually easy to

install. Sliding shelves are great for items you need to access often: such as spatulas, can openers, stirrers and other items. By having the shelf slide out, what's on the shelf is instantly visible and reaching for something is more convenient.

2. **Use air-tight containers for dry goods—and label them.** You've seen these kinds of containers in the kitchen organizer section of your favorite store. They're perfect for keeping bread crumbs, flour, sugar and other dry goods stored as well as fresh. Make them more organized by creating self-stick identification labels using an electronic labelmaker. You can even print your labels in colors to differentiate your dry goods into color-coded categories.

3. **Install racks on the insides of kitchen doors.** Compact hanging rack systems, usually constructed of either sturdy plastic or molded metal wire, are available in most supermarkets, department stores and home improvement stores. These affix with a few screws to the inside of kitchen closet doors, pantry doors and cabinet doors— and they're ideal for holding and organizing brooms, dust pans, plastic and foil wraps, spice jars, coffee tins and many other kitchen necessities.

4. **Utilize the underside of wall cabinets.** If your kitchen is like most, counter space is at a premium. Help keep the space free and clear by installing kitchen appliances that are specially designed to hang from underneath wall

cabinets. Toaster ovens, compact microwaves, coffee pots, and many other small "electrics" are all available with hanging design. Another benefit: these types of appliances may be easier to use because in most instances they will be installed at approximately eye level.

5. **Place cleaning supplies all in a single bucket.** Store rubber gloves, cleaning agents, scrub brushes and other kitchen cleaning items all together in one bucket and place the bucket in the cabinet underneath your sink. Whenever it's time to clean, you'll only have to look in one place for all the cleaning liquids and tools you need.

Going Back to School Is as Easy as 1, 2, 3

It's September and you know what that means: shopping for school supplies, a new outfit for the first day and rearranging everyone's schedule.

But, there is more to going back to school than new clothes, freshly sharpened pencils and clean notebooks. Back-to-school time is about becoming organized, staying focused and gaining knowledge. Here are ten tips to ease the transition.

1. **Locker lockdown:** A locker is more than a place to display your favorite pictures; it's a place to stop between classes to organize your thoughts and your schoolwork. Arrange your locker in a logical fashion. Try keeping your notebooks with the corresponding books, folders

and other collateral materials. "If you tend to accumulate trash in your storage space, keep a mini garbage can or small plastic bag in your locker to help keep this area clean and organized."

2. **Location, location, location:** Where you study is equally as important as how you study. Studying in front of the TV, in a noisy room or a place with poor lighting makes studying an arduous task. Find a well-lit, quiet area in which to conduct your studies. You will find that if you work in a conducive and relaxing area, the task will be much easier.

3. **Time management:** Procrastination takes hold of all of us at some point. To combat the urge to be a couch potato, I recommend managing your time wisely with the help of a schedule. At the beginning of each week, make a timetable. Block out a certain amount of your free time for schoolwork. As you get daily assignments, split your designated school time accordingly. This tactic will put you on a regular schedule, which will effectively cut back on time spent dawdling.

4. **Study in groups:** At the beginning of each school year, set up study groups. Each person has strengths that can complement the study habits and learning potential of the rest of the group. By forming a group early in the year, you can form a working relationship with your peers. Often, someone may have picked up on an important piece of information that you missed. If you put

your minds together, you will be able to see the whole picture of what your teacher wants you to know.

5. **Jump start the school year:** Before the school year begins and the workload gets too heavy, talk to your teachers about reading assignments. If you can, read some of the books over the summer that you will be required to read during the year. This will lighten up your workload and make your school year less stressful. When it comes time to read those books in class, refresh your memory by reading a study guide. This tactic helps you to not only avoid some stress during the school year but also helps you to retain the knowledge. If you read the books without having to worry about how many other assignments you have to do, then you will be able to focus on the materials at hand.

6. **Get energized:** Start your day with a good night's sleep and a healthy breakfast. Begin each day well-rested and well-fed, and you will be focused and ready to learn.

7. **Plan ahead:** As soon as you receive your class schedule, mark all due dates, test dates and other important days on your calendar. Keep track of when things need to be done. If you keep a running list of important dates, you can plan accordingly if something comes up. This way, you will be prepared for the year.

8. **Organize your wardrobe:** Time is tighter during the school year, so make things easier on yourself by organizing your wardrobe over the summer. Clean and

straighten your closets and drawers, prepare your back-
pack and school clothes, and list any items that might
need to be replaced or repaired so that you are ready for
the school year.

9. **Take complete notes:** Most students only take notes
   about the subject matter, but never think of recording
   what the teacher says he or she is looking for from their
   pupils. Keep a small notebook handy and jot down notes
   when the teacher talks about an assignment, mentions
   class participation or discusses deadlines. If you write
   down what your teacher expects, you will never be
   caught unprepared again. Keep the notebook handy as
   an easy referencing tool for doing schoolwork or studying for an exam.

10. **Get involved:** Set time aside for extracurricular activi-
    ties. Get involved in athletics, creative clubs, drama club,
    the football team, yearbook or anything else that might
    interest you. This is a great way to make friends, relieve
    tension and relax, all while doing something productive.
    Most importantly, get excited about going back to
    school. Start the school year off with a positive attitude
    and you will be fully prepared to learn and enjoy your-
    self while doing so.

Dear Sharon,

My daughter is about to complete elementary school and in the fall she will be moving up to middle school. I wanted to get a jump on her supplies, before the crunch in August when everyone else will pack the stores looking for back-to-school items. My daughter's always had a tough time staying organized. Is there something she can use both in school and also at home to keep track of her assignments and other "stuff"?

Gwen

Dear Gwen,

I have the ideal solution. It's called the Oxford 8 Pocket Organizer and it's perfect for organizing subjects as well as transporting homework and other assignments to and from school. This product has eight individual pockets to divide school subjects. Another solution to keep all of her subjects organized is to color match folders to text books. Use color stretchable book covers with matching pocket portfolios and ring binders.

Now that you have successfully completed the book, you should be well on your way to being organized and getting your ACT together. I hope the articles in the book have given you the insights you need to put you on your way to leading a more organized and less stressful life. We all deal with enough stress in

our lives without having to add to it with clutter and disorgani-
zation. I will leave you with a final tip: Reward yourself for each
job well done. You deserve it.

Now that you've finished *I Hate Filing*, you should be in a better position to tackle the organizational challenges that crop up
in you life. One last tip; practice what you've learned and make
it part of life's daily routine. You now have the tools and tips to
help get your ACT together and I hope this book will help you
achieve organization bliss and reach those goals that are important to you.

Have an Organization Question?

If you're in an organization mess (literally!) and want to ask
for Sharon's help in solving it, contact *www.pendaflex.com*.

NOTES

NOTES

The Senior Organizer

PERSONAL

MEDICAL

LEGAL

FINANCIAL

Organizing for a better quality of life

Debby S. Bitticks
Lynn Benson
Dorothy K. Breininger

Code #4893 • paperback • $16.95

No more digging through files! *The Senior Organizer* is an all-in-one workbook for a senior's vital information: personal, medical, legal and financial.

The Dog Diet

A MEMOIR

What My Dog Taught Me
About Shedding Pounds, Licking Stress and
Getting a New Leash on Life

PATTI LAWSON

Code #3943 • hardcover • $16.95

Boy does Ms. Lawson know dogs! Fantastic book for dog lovers and anyone who want to stay in shape—and lighten up their lives to boot!

—Richard Simmons

THE TEN
COMMITMENTS
Translating Good Intentions into Great Choices

DAVID SIMON, M.D.

Code #4060 • hardcover • $16.95

In this fascinating and uniquely insightful book, David explores the core tenets of Western spiritual values and demonstrates how, with a subtle yet powerful shift in perception, the essential truths of East and West merge to create a compelling vision for a better world.

—Deepak Chopra

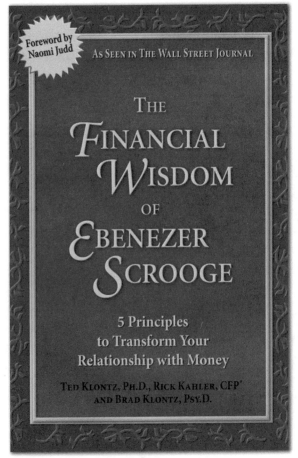